ONE
REALITY:
THE
HARMONY
OF
SCIENCE
AND
RELIGION

Introduction by John S. Hatcher

COMPILED BY BONNIE J. TAYLOR

Bahá'í
PUBLISHING

Wilmette, Illinois

Bahá'í Publishing
401 Greenleaf Avenue, Wilmette, Illinois 60091-2844

Copyright © 2013 by the National Spiritual Assembly of
the Bahá'ís of the United States

16   15   14   13   4   3   2   1

Library of Congress Cataloging-in-Publication Data
One reality : the harmony of science and religion / compiled by
Bonnie J. Taylor ; introduction by John S. Hatcher.
    pages cm
 Includes bibliographical references.
 ISBN 978-1-61851-049-5 (alk. paper)
 1. Religion and science. 2. Bahai Faith—Doctrines. I. Taylor,
Bonnie J., editor of compilation.
 BL240.3.O55 2013
 297.9'3165—dc23
                                        2013021058

Cover design by Pepper Oldziey
Book design by Patrick Falso

CONTENTS

PREFACE

One Reality offers a Bahá'í perspective on the subject of the harmony of science and religion. The extracts contained in this compilation come from the following sources:

The writings of Bahá'u'lláh (1817–1892), the Prophet and Founder of the Bahá'í Faith.

The writings and recorded utterances of 'Abdu'l-Bahá (1844–1921), the son and appointed successor of Bahá'u'lláh, regarded by Bahá'ís as the authorized interpreter of his Father's writings and the Perfect Exemplar of the Faith's teachings.

Letters written by, and on behalf of, Shoghi Effendi (1897–1957), the Guardian of the Bahá'í Faith. Shoghi Effendi was the grandson of 'Abdu'l-Bahá and served as the head of the Faith from 'Abdu'l-Bahá's passing in 1921 until his own passing in 1957.

Letters written by, and on behalf of, the Universal House of Justice, the international governing body of the Bahá'í Faith. The Universal House of Justice, first elected in 1963, was ordained in the writings of Bahá'u'lláh and is elected every five years by the Bahá'ís of the world.

INTRODUCTION:
SCIENCE, RELIGION,
AND REALITY

*The spiritual world is like unto the phenomenal world.
They are the exact counterpart of each other. Whatever
objects appear in this world of existence are the outer
pictures of the world of heaven.*

—'Abdu'l-Bahá,
The Promulgation of Universal Peace, p. 12

Since the schism between science and religion began in the Western World during the later Middle Ages, the divide has widened to the point of becoming an all-out war, the ravages of which still afflict us. The enduring result is that at one extreme, people of science are presumed to be "Godless nonbelievers" who view the world as a complex but entirely material mechanism run according to discoverable and incontrovertible physical laws and principles. Followers of various religious traditions, on the other hand, tend to view reality as divided into two distinct and often contradictory realms—the material realm and the heavenly spiritual realm.

CAN'T WE ALL JUST GET ALONG?

We are all too familiar with the panoply of issues that presently divide society as fallout from this contention. For example, how we view the question of a woman's right to choose versus the civil rights of the unborn child may depend largely on our belief about whether there is a soul that distinguishes human life from animal life, a spiritual essence that begins sometime during the process of conception.

Courts may uphold laws based on the notion of "viability" as determined by medical science, but advancements in medical technology render this decision amorphous. Viability is becoming increasingly early in the gestation process, and the only logical solution must derive from the answer to the more encompassing question regarding the source of our human reality. Are we the product of what our brain can do, or is there something that "runs" the brain from without—a soul, an essentially metaphysical "self" that characterizes us as essentially human from the start?

In like manner, the tension continues in the conflicting views between those who advocate a strict materialist view of the emergence of human life through random chance mutation and those who believe that a Higher Power intervened directly to cause creation to come about. Of course, there is the possibility of some sort of reconciliation were some theory capable of synthesizing scientific evidence of evolution with the possibility of "external" or metaphysical influence. For example, possibly we human beings did evolve, but are not merely chance mutations. Could it be that we evolved, but were always a distinct creation inherently capable of ascending to our present condition? In other words, perhaps God exists but has employed some form of evolution as a tool with which to bring about human life on planet Earth.

Allied to this issue is the further question as to whether or not this Creator continues to oversee His creation. If there is a God, does He still provide continuous guidance for the advancement of society by periodic intervention in human history? Even more precisely, is there some discernible, logical, and systematic method by which this guidance is revealed and implemented? And, finally, if God exists, is He a "personal" God aware of our thoughts and problems and concerned with the well-being of each and every one of us?

Another contemporary example of conflict deriving from this tension between scientific and religious views of reality is the "Big Bang" theory, at least as it is proposed as being the source of the entirety of reality. Opposed to this idea that reality as a whole (both physical and metaphysical dimensions) began by chance at a certain locus at a specific point in time (approximately fourteen billion years ago) are theories that incorporate a metaphysical concept of intentionality in whatever process or processes instigated the portion of reality we are presently able to detect, given the limitations of present-day technology. Additionally, even if what we can presently observe is the result of a Big Bang, should we assume it was the first and only such phenomenon? Could there not have been previous Big Bangs? And if the universe is infinite, could there not be other Big Bangs occurring at this very moment?

The "Big Bang" is a big boon for the scientific community in providing what seems to be an inclusive and conclusive solution to the query about how reality came into being, as well as providing comfortable limitations about the age and size of reality. But it leaves in its wake many lingering questions, and not solely for those who advocate belief in a Creator.

For example, how does this theory account for the origin of energy sufficient to cause such an explosion transmuting this massive force into material forms of solar systems, galaxies, and collections of galaxies? And if reality emanated from that time and point, into what did it expand, unless we accept that space itself was created as matter expanded? And is there truly nothing beyond the matter at the leading edge of this ongoing event, many billions of light years away?

But the overriding question regarding any strictly materialist theory of creation is how an amazingly complex order came about, such as presently exists on planet Earth. Are we the single propitious accident among a virtually infinite array of planets in creation?

And even given a fairly vast amount of time for this chance "order" to come about, does not this propitious sequence occur in complete contravention of all expected scientific probability. According to Roger Penrose in *The Large, the Small, and the Human Mind*,[1] for human life to evolve randomly would require the probability of one chance in ten to the power of one hundred and twenty-three. According to the second law of thermodynamics, in an isolated or closed system, we should expect greater entropy or disorder to be occurring. But what we find on our planet is quite the opposite—increasing order and complexity, an improbable or unscientific result without the inclusion of some as yet unexplained "ordering" force. Or as I explain this improbable result more precisely elsewhere,

> The second law of thermodynamics has several equivalent formulations, one of the simplest and clearest being that order or complexity of structure is improbable while disorder or simplicity of structure is probable. For though virtually any configuration might represent disorder, only a limited number of configurations can be said to represent order. Thus, when we apply this principle to evolution [or to the emergence of human life on our planet], we must carefully distinguish

---

1. *The Large, the Small, and the Human Mind* (Cambridge University Press, 1999), p. 48.

fact from theory. The fact of evolution is the persistent emergence over time (about 600 million years) of increasingly complex forms of structures of life, a phenomenon that represents a persistent movement from disorder to order—therefore from the probable toward the improbable. Any viable *theory* of evolution must be capable of explaining this fact.[2]

And there are other equally vital disputes that derive from these two ostensibly contradictory perspectives about reality. Some involve relatively discrete areas of concern—for example, does the physical act of prayer have a metaphysical influence on physical events (a problem to which materialists respond with the axiom that action at a distance is impossible)? Is supplication to God simply a religious exercise, the effects of which are exclusively emotional and psychological, or can our thoughts and will produce physical outcomes, most especially when empowered by divine assistance?

Perhaps the most evocative question related to these contrary theories of reality concerns the matter of personhood or "self." Is our self-consciousness, together with our other "mental" powers, the result of material mechanisms and processes emanating spontaneously

---

2. John Hatcher, *Close Connections: The Bridge between Spiritual and Physical Reality* (Wilmette, IL: Bahá'í Publishing, 2005), pp. 98–99.

from the human brain quite beyond our willful control? Or is there the possibility that self-consciousness, willpower, and other distinctly human capacities emanate from a metaphysical source, a soul? If this latter scenario is possible, then the actual "self" is not contained within the body-brain, but is non-local, maintaining a temporary associative relationship with the body-brain, analogous, perhaps, to a "gamer's" dexterous control of an avatar in a computer game.

Of course, we should also mention another major concern we have about our personal reality related to this same question—whether or not there is life after death. Are we destined to enter a realm similar to that portrayed in so-called "near death experiences"? Do these vividly recalled out-of-body encounters with the afterlife accurately portray reality as we will experience it once we are no longer constrained by our association with this physical apparatus that is our body? Or, as many neuroscientists assert, are these experiences merely hallucinations devised by our oxygen-deprived brains as they attempt to comfort themselves against the reality of impending demise?

There are numerous other specific questions that also hinge on our view of the nature and the structure of reality. For example, is there really a "God particle," some finally indivisible building-block of creation? Or is it possible that materiality, by definition, is necessarily composite and, therefore, infinitely divisible.

An entire field of interest that is similarly dependent on this division between perspectives relates to what we think is the source of ideas about morality and human virtue. Are moral concepts and spiritual attributes merely imaginative creations devised by those in power to control others? Or do moral imperatives have an actual basis in reality? Do virtues, spiritual attributes, and spiritual capacities exist quite apart from whether or not we personally choose to understand and acquire them? And is our individual and collective quest for justice and peace merely a practical but arbitrary solution to complex social issues? Or do we humans possess some inherent notion of spiritual principles derived from our soul or from the divine guidance we receive directly and indirectly from a spiritual realm?

Let it suffice for now to note that great thinkers have composed many volumes examining these and similar issues, the solutions to which seem wedged between these two antithetical views of reality. Similarly, numerous studies have also traced the origin and historical evolution of this contention between science and religion. And one central observation we discover in these studies is that this division of human thought becomes much more virulent as even the "great minds" and their supporters become insistent about their particular observations and, subsequently, resistant to evidence that would suggest opposing points of view.

The conflict also becomes more vehement as successive religions have become staid, dogmatic, and intractable. This tension has become especially pronounced now that science has become entirely freed from the needless constraints that past religious authority imposed so that enlightened minds can explore freely whatever they wish, and arrive at whatever seem to be the most logical results of replicable experimentation.

REALITY *IS* WHAT REALITY *IS*

If we attempt to view this conflict with a degree of objectivity, we can, without being too condescending, detect a certain degree of silliness in the intransigence of both sides. After all, the single objective among the learned members of our human family should always be the same—to discover and share the truth about our own nature, about the environment in which we presently abide, and about the nature and structure of reality as a whole. And if those who take a scientific/materialist stand become obdurate in their rejection of the possibility that there might be a metaphysical aspect to reality, then the progress of human knowledge is hindered quite as much as it is by those who reject science out of hand when its observations appear to conflict with belief in a soul, a Creator, or a spiritual realm.

The point is that reality *is* what it *is*, regardless of what we would like it to be. Consequently, when we allow our examination of reality to become slanted toward a personal goal—the victory of an ideology rather than the discovery of truth—then advancing our understanding of reality becomes encumbered or possibly deterred altogether.

The Bahá'í belief is not that science and religion *should* be unified but rather that reality is a single organic creation, and that any conflict in our conclusions about its nature is an indication of flaws in our study of reality rather than flaws in reality itself. The Bahá'í view presumes that once this fact becomes understood and accepted, all branches of study of the relationship between science and religion can collaborate in discovering how the dimensions of reality function as integral parts of a single organism.

Along the lines of this same theme, 'Abdu'l-Bahá—the son of Bahá'u'lláh, the Prophet and Founder of the Bahá'í Faith—observes that the methodology for all studies of reality should employ the same rigorous standards, regardless of what part of reality is being examined. For example, he notes, religious beliefs that are contrary to the standards of the scientific method are fragile assumptions that ultimately falter and fail: "If religious beliefs and opinions are found contrary to the standards of science they are mere superstitions and imaginations; for the antithesis of knowledge is ignorance, and the child of ignorance is superstition" (*The Promulgation of Universal Peace*, p. 251).

Obviously this same axiom applies to the study of material reality as a field unto itself. For while we might think that the logical demands of empiricism and the need to substantiate findings with replicable evidence might render material sciences immune to bias or insistence on a personal point of view, we know full well from the history of science that such is not the case. For example, we can observe such resistance to change in the attempt to devise convoluted additions to the Ptolemaic model of reality in order to account for increasing evidence that it was an inaccurate or inadequate description of the cosmos.

A somewhat more recent example of the same tendency at work can be considered in reviewing some of the theories that were derived from the famous Michelson-Morley light experiment in 1887. This ingenious experiment was intended to calculate how much effect the ether wave had on the speed of light. The presumption was that the light traveling with the ether wave would have a greater speed because the speed of the medium (the ether) through which the light passed would be additional to the speed that light inherently possesses.

The results seemed to indicate that the speed of light was the same in any direction and constant from any frame of reference. These results were employed by Einstein in his conclusion that the speed of light is the one constant in the universe. Still another conclusion, though perhaps a needless one, was that the theoretical ether must not exist.

Recently both of these theories have been questioned as the result of further experimentation and study. At the particle accelerator at the Cern laboratory in Switzerland an image of the Higgs boson particle, also called the "God particle," was made. Theoretically, this is the smallest expression of material composition. Also at Cern an experiment with the Hadron accelerator seemed to indicate that some particulates were exceeding the speed of light. Whether either of these findings turns out to be finally correct, what the ongoing study demonstrates is that all knowledge we acquire is a work in progress. The truth about reality will always be relative.

Consequently, we must now consider the fact that something might exceed the speed of light, especially if matter is infinitely divisible. In other words, if the material realm is made of "stuff," then there can be no part of it that is not composite. Therefore, might we not theorize that there could be an "ether" that is so refined it has no influence on photons of light? Indeed, 'Abdu'l-Bahá makes statements in a tablet that has been only provisionally translated (the Tablet of the Universe) to the effect that there is no absolute void in physical reality, that the entirety of the physical realm is composite, and that every composition swims about in a sea of materiality more refined than itself.[3]

FORTUNATELY REALITY IS LOGICAL
The Bahá'í view of reality is not derived from dogma or ideology, but rather from the belief that both dimensions of reality—physical and metaphysical—are

---

3. The "Tablet of the Universe," can be found in its original Persian form in *Makatib-i Abdu'l-Bahá, vol. 1,* pp. 13–32.

logically structured, function in a coherent counter-part relationship, and thus can be examined and de-scribed as a single organic system. Therefore, before reading this compilation, we would do well to con-sider a brief overview of some fundamental Bahá'í axioms to which the selected passages allude.

As we have implied, one major axiom about reality we find in the Bahá'í writings is that creation is not an accident. This axiom would seem to be supported by all the evidence regarding the evolution of life on our planet, including human life as the fruit of that process. As we have already noted, this process demonstrates a complete violation of the laws of probability. Accord-ing to logic and scientific laws, order, complexification, and progressive refinement should not emerge from molten hot chaos. The exact opposite should happen. Furthermore, the law of parsimony requires that, given a choice, we opt for the simplest logical theory. In the case of our planet, the most logical explanation is that some "outside" force (outside the physical universe—"meta-physical") has exerted sufficient intelligent or propitious influence to bring about human beings and, by degrees, a highly sophisticated, if presently quarrel-some, human global civilization.

Another foundational Bahá'í view of the logic of reality is that the benign and moral concepts underly-ing our present vision of a peaceful and just society derive from the same source that has kept our world from falling apart, a metaphysical consciousness of power and beneficence, a cognitive Being Whose existence is discernible and demonstrable if we know what we are looking for, where to search, and what tools to employ in that search.

The Bahá'í writings expand this assertion by explaining that there is a Creator, a God, Who, while essentially unknowable (we cannot detect the essence of this Being with our senses or comprehend the totality of His mind or will), is imminently "knowable" in terms of His attributes and powers. These are plainly manifest in every aspect of physical creation, an axiom Bahá'u'lláh notes in the following statement: "From the exalted source, and out of the essence of His favor and bounty He hath entrusted every created thing with a sign of His knowledge, so that none of His creatures may be deprived of its share in expressing, each according to its capacity and rank, this knowledge" (*Gleanings from the Writings of Bahá'u'lláh,* no. 124.2). But of course, only as we learn how to discern symbolic and metaphorical expressions of reality embodied in nature, and in the natural laws that bind nature together, can we acquire this knowledge.

Another major verity in the Bahá'í teachings helps to explain why the Creator would desire to create anything in the first place. According to the Founders of all the revealed world religions, the Creator is loving, beneficent, and entirely altruistic in all His motives. Therefore, it is His desire to share the bounty of knowing Him and establishing a relationship with Him with a being that has the capacity to discern His existence and then to translate that knowledge into words and action.

Stated more directly, the nature of the being with which the Creator wishes to establish a love relationship needs to be capable of abstract thought and should have sufficient free will to choose to participate in this relationship. Otherwise, if this relationship were coerced or imposed by the Creator, then while the Creator, like a loving parent, might have unconditional love for us, this would not truly be a love relationship inasmuch as a relationship is bilateral and reciprocal.

Yet another insight related to the Creator's goal in this continuous process is that for this relationship to become instigated and sustained, there needs to emanate from God some form of guidance in the form of a Messenger or Teacher to explain and model this process for us. Since we human beings have no inherent knowledge of how this might be accomplished, God empowers Beings, Whom the Bahá'í writings designate as "Manifestations," to have innate knowledge of reality and to possess the capacity to advance the human spiritual condition by creating social structures that give expression to both dimensions of reality.

For example, the Manifestations provide knowledge about how the soul is the source of our humanity and how our free will makes us responsible for using our capacity for abstract thought to recognize these Teachers when They appear. As a sign of our understanding and a completion of the act of learning, we are then admonished to follow whatever guidance the Manifestations design us as a path for enriching our lives and refining our character.

Finally, the Bahá'í teachings affirm that inasmuch as the Creator is infinite, changeless, and eternal, the Creator's desire to fashion human beings for the purpose of this love relationship was not a sudden impulse. Logically, since the Creator is eternal and this desire has always been an inseparable part of His nature, then we must also conclude that creation itself, including human beings, is likewise eternal. The worlds of God, whether metaphysical or physical, are infinite. None is limited by time, space, or plentitude, even though the entire system is in a constant state of change and motion, the Big Bang in our part of the universe being one example of such creative processes.

WHY REALITY IS COMPRISED OF A DUAL NATURE

These fundamental propositions that constitute some major axioms about the Bahá'í view of reality lead us to what might be the most central Bahá'í perspective, that there is a collaborative and complementary relationship between the dual dimensions of reality. This theory explains the cause of the division between science and religion, and yet it also establishes the basis for the resolution of this conflict.

By affirming that there are twin expressions of a single system, one physical and the other metaphysical, this Bahá'í concept of a purposeful complimentary relationship affirms that each perspective helps explain the other: "The spiritual world is like unto the phenomenal world. They are the exact counterpart of each other.

Whatever objects appear in this world of existence are the outer pictures of the world of heaven" ('Abdu'l-Bahá, *The Promulgation of Universal Peace,* p. 12).

As we have noted, this counterpart relationship does not mean these twin dimensions are coequal. The purpose of the physical dimension is to provide us sensible expressions and experiences as the foundation for our comprehension of the divine realm. Thus, the twin expressions of reality are alluded to with distinctly different terminology. The spiritual realm is referred to with such epithets as "the Kingdom on high," "the Kingdom of God," "the Kingdom of Heaven," while the material expression of creation is characterized as "the kingdom of names and attributes," "the kingdom of creation," "the kingdom of earth," and so on.

But the central premise regarding both realms in this "counterpart" relationship is that the material realm is devised by the Creator as a classroom or workshop wherein we are taught to recognize and thereby understand the metaphorical or symbolic expressions of the unseen dimension as it becomes manifest in metaphorical or symbolic terms. Thus as we follow this path to enlightenment, we also come to appreciate that both the spiritual and the physical aspects of creation are designed as coherent dimensions of a single reality, the whole of which is devised to assist us in advancing an increasingly refined love relationship with the Creator.

Though implicit, it is well worth repeating that in this educational process, the physical realm constitutes our first introduction to metaphysical reality, and yet it is clearly the metaphysical realm that has primacy in this relationship. The same can be said to be true for our personal or individual reality. While we are first aware of ourselves as physical beings, it is our spiritual essence, our soul, that is the origin and principal expression of "self." As we have noted, from a Bahá'í perspective, the soul is the source from which emanate such essential powers as understanding, will-power, persistence, and reflection.

Therefore, while physical appearance, extreme wealth, and vast power are most often touted as the prized objectives for human attainment by society at large, the progress in the continuation of our lives beyond this mortal realm will be predicated on the spiritual insight and divine powers we have attained. This objective is accomplished, the Bahá'í writings attest, when we employ physical practices for the realization of spiritual enterprises. Foremost among these objectives is a progressively more refined, world-encompassing social structure, the foundation for which is, and will remain, the morally refined family in a spiritually collaborative community.

MUTUAL DISCOVERY OF OURSELVES

With this minimal background information about the Bahá'í view of reality, we can appreciate that for the Bahá'í, the study of reality is not confined to any particular field. All areas of investigation alike can be valuable paths to understanding the coherence of creation. It is precisely from this point of view that the unity of science and religion need not be imposed or coerced. As we have already noted, the unity among all branches of human learning is an established fact if reality itself, while multidimensional, is organically whole. Therefore, any given area of investigation constitutes a useful vector of knowledge, like a beam of light illuminating some facet of this complex system.

Consequently, it might be naïve and ludicrous to suggest that the solution to the divide between science and religion should come about simply by encouraging students of science and students of religion to be more collegial. No, the underlying principle of the Bahá'í notion of the unity of science and religion is that over the course of time, every field of study will inevitably discover its relationship to every other field as, step-by-step, all fields of human understanding become collaborative. Strict materialists who reject the notion of a metaphysical aspect to reality, or at least the interplay between these dimensions, be they particle physicists or astrophysicists, will eventually discover the metaphysical system that the cosmos mimes for us. The students of human nature, likewise, will in time discover the manner in which the human brain channels the distinctly human powers of the soul.

Even now there are numerous examples we could cite where this coherence of learning is taking place. Several oncologists with whom I have conversed have come to accept the existence of a metaphysical reality, an afterlife, as daily these physicians observe their terminally ill patients who, inexorably and progressively approaching the end of this life, have reassuring visions of an afterlife and dialogues with relatives who await them on the "other side."

Similarly, some contemporary scientists dedicated to the study of the human brain have come to view this most complex of physical mechanisms as a transceiver for some metaphysical source (a soul or mind) external to the "meat between our ears":

> In science, we have largely ignored how consciousness manifests in our existence. We've done this by assuming that the brain produces consciousness, although how it might do so has never been explained and can hardly be imagined. The polite term for this trick is "emergence." At a certain stage of biological complexity, evolutionary biologists claim, consciousness pops out of the brain like a rabbit from a magician's hat. Yet this claim rests on no direct evidence whatsoever. As Rutgers University philosopher Jerry A. Fodo flatly states, "Nobody has the slightest idea how anything material could be conscious. So much for our philosophy of consciousness."[4]

---

4. Larry Dossey, *The Science of Premonitions,* p. 189. Dossey further observes: "Others suggest that there are no mental states at all, such as love, courage, or patriotism, but only electrochemical brain fluxes that should not be described with such inflated language. They dismiss thoughts and beliefs for the same reasons. This led Nobel neurophysiologist Sir John Eccles to remark that 'professional philosophers and psychologists think up the notion that there are no thoughts, come to believe that there

A metaphysical essence, they have concluded, is effectively a more likely explanation for the emanation of abstract thought, acts of will, the non-locality of memory, and self-consciousness than is the strictly materialist explanation that these capacities result from the systematic but autonomous firing of a hundred billion neurons.

A number of studies, such as those by Dr. Larry Dossey, MD, have demonstrated the positive effects of prayer on seriously ill patients. Likewise, the power of the human will to affect physical outcomes in a predictable and replicable pattern was demonstrated in the highly regarded Princeton study by Jahn and Dunne as detailed in *The Margins of Reality: The Role of Consciousness in the Physical World.* This well-documented study, as well as Dossey's work on prayer, are but two examples of science having to call into question the long-standing materialist axiom that action at a distance is not possible or that human consciousness cannot originate from a non-local source. Indeed, the idea of human will is a problem for the strict materialist who is forced to devise some

---

are no beliefs, and feel strongly that there are no feelings.' Eccles was emphasizing the absurdities that have crept into the debates about consciousness. They are not hard to spot. Some of the oddest experiences I recall are attending conferences where one speaker after another employs his consciousness to denounce the existence of consciousness, ignoring the fact that he consciously chose to register for the meeting, make travel plans, prepare his talks, and so on."

explanation for this otherwise metaphysical force in terms of quantum physics.[5]

Perhaps the most persistent and consistent evidence influencing formerly materialist scientists to accept the possibility of a metaphysical dimension to reality are the increasing number of convincingly chronicled near death experiences (NDEs) or out-of-body experiences (OBEs). The work begun in the 1970s and 80s by Elisabeth Kübler-Ross and Raymond Mood, MD, has continued unabated and largely intact. Most recently in the best-selling autobiographically based account *Proof of Heaven: A Neurosurgeon's Journey into the Afterlife* (Simon and Schuster, 2012), Dr. Eben Alexander describes in detail how he changed his opinion from a "scientific" or materialist explanation for the NDE to a "metaphysical" or "spiritual" explanation:

> I grew up in a scientific world, the son of a neurosurgeon. I followed my father's path and became an academic neurosurgeon, teaching at Harvard Medical School and other universities. I understand what happens to the brain when people are near death, and I had always believed there were good scientific explanations for the heavenly out-of-body journeys described by those who narrowly escaped death. (interview)

5. See David M. Wegner, *The Illusion of Conscious Will* (Cambridge, Mass: MIT Press, 2002).

Alexander goes on to provide a narrative about his coma and the subsequent experiences that completely defied any rational explanation other than what the experience revealed to him, that there is a spiritual reality. He explains how his experience provided him with indisputable evidence that the destiny of the human "self" or "soul" is to enter a spiritual realm once the illusion of being entirely physical is removed at the dissociation between the conscious soul and the human temple.

STITCHING REALITY TOGETHER

The final and possibly the most profound insight the reader might require in order to grasp the foundation of Bahá'í-based studies regarding the nature of reality has to do with the Bahá'í belief regarding how the twin dimensions of reality—the physical and the spiritual—are effectively "joined and knit together."

As we have noted, from a Bahá'í perspective, there is nothing in existence that does not have something to demonstrate to us about the unseen realm, if we are attentive to what it is we are seeking. For example, Bahá'u'lláh observes, "Within every blade of grass are enshrined the mysteries of an inscrutable Wisdom, and upon every rosebush a myriad nightingales pour out, in blissful rapture, their melody" (*Gleanings from the Writings of Bahá'u'lláh,* no. 125.9).

From this perspective of the inherent purpose and unity of creation, we have no need to figure out how to conjoin these twin expressions of reality. They are already unified in a counterpart relationship. It is, instead, our task to advance our understanding of how this present physical environment we inhabit reflects and explains to us the essential reality that is the spiritual realm. Then, as we make progress in uncovering truths about this relationship, we can apply our knowledge to useful practices in our collective task of creating what Bahá'u'lláh alludes to as "an ever-advancing civilization."

As we noted earlier, however, there is a logical and inescapable need for us to receive external guidance in our study of reality. We can't simply intuit all we need to know to accomplish our God-given objectives. Thus when Christ exhorts His followers to pray that the kingdom of God become manifest on earth, even as it is in heaven, there is in the revealed laws and moral principles He articulates explicit guidance about the part His own followers can play in the realization of this process.

In the subsequent unfolding of religious history, this advice has been reiterated and advanced through the revealed teachings of Muḥammad, the Báb, and most recently Bahá'u'lláh. By means of this progressive enlightenment, coupled with the evermore expansive social practices that these Manifestations introduce and mandate, we can participate in forging our planet into a spiritually based community. But this progress on our part has depended and always will depend on divine assistance from these Messengers or "Manifestations."

It is through these Beings Who appear periodically throughout history that the course of human civilization advances. More to the point, it is the Bahá'í belief that it is precisely through the successive and progressive guidance of these specialized Beings that the two realms (or two aspects of creation) become increasingly similar so that our earthly society over time will fulfill Christ's behest that our planet progressively mirror forth the attributes of the divine world.

In one of the daily prayers revealed by Bahá'u'lláh, the supplicant recites the following verity about this power of the Prophets of God to show us how to "join and knit together" these twin expressions of divine creation in such a way that our planet, like a cell in the universal body of creation, will gradually participate in giving life to the whole of reality:

> I testify unto that whereunto have testified all created things, and the Concourse on high, and the inmates of the all-highest Paradise, and beyond them the Tongue of Grandeur itself from the all-glorious Horizon, that Thou art God, that there is no God but Thee, and that He Who hath been manifested is the Hidden Mystery, the Treasured Symbol, through Whom the letters B and E (Be) have been joined and knit together. (Bahá'u'lláh, *Prayers and Meditations,* p. 320)

The imperative "Be!" in this context symbolizes the Creator's expression of His ceaseless desire that reality be brought into being. But at the heart of the Creator's plan for this process to become realized is the advent of the Manifestations. By means of this explicit design for the advancement of human civilization, spiritual attributes gradually become conjoined with social practices and structures to form in time a global commonwealth. It is this spiritually based global community capable of endless development and limitless refinement that represents the Bahá'í view of the Creator's purpose for planet Earth, even as it is the limitless refinement of each individual that represents the culmination of the eternal journey of each individual soul.

John S. Hatcher, Professor Emeritus

Chapter One

THE PRINCIPLE
OF THE HARMONY OF
SCIENCE AND RELIGION

He [Bahá'u'lláh] proclaims that religion must be in harmony with science and reason. . . . The harmony of religious belief with reason is a new vista which Bahá'u'lláh has opened for the soul of man.

—'Abdu'l-Bahá,
The Promulgation of Universal Peace, p. 641

O God, O Thou Who hast cast Thy splendor over the luminous realities of men, shedding upon them the resplendent lights of knowledge and guidance, and hast chosen them out of all created things for this supernal grace, and hast caused them to encompass all things, to understand their inmost essence, and to disclose their mysteries, bringing them forth out of darkness into the visible world! "He verily showeth His special mercy to whomsoever He will." O Lord, help Thou Thy loved ones to acquire knowledge and the sciences and arts, and to unravel the secrets that are treasured up in the inmost reality of all created beings. Make them to hear the hidden truths that are written and embedded in the heart of all that is. Make them to be ensigns of guidance amongst all creatures, and piercing rays of the mind shedding forth their light in this, the "first life." Make them to be leaders unto Thee, guides unto Thy path, runners urging men on to Thy Kingdom.

Thou verily art the Powerful, the Protector, the Potent, the Defender, the Mighty, the Most Generous. ('Abdu'l-Bahá, in *The Compilation of Compilations, vol. I,* pp. 251–52.)

SOME INTRODUCTORY PASSAGES

The Tablets of Bahá'u'lláh are many. The precepts and teachings they contain are universal, covering every subject. He has revealed scientific explanations ranging throughout all the realms of human inquiry and investigation—astronomy, biology, medical science, etc. In the Kitáb-i-Íqán He has given expositions of the meanings of the Gospel and other heavenly Books. He wrote lengthy Tablets upon civilization, sociology and government. Every subject is considered. ('Abdu'l-Bahá, *The Promulgation of Universal Peace,* p. 215.)

The Bahá'í Faith recognizes the unity of God of His Prophets, upholds the principle of an unfettered search after truth, condemns all forms of superstition and prejudice, teaches that the fundamental purpose of religion is to promote concord and harmony, that it must go hand-in-hand with science, and that it constitutes the sole and ultimate basis of a peaceful, an ordered and progressive society. It inculcates the principle of equal opportunity, rights and privileges for both sexes, advocates compulsory education, abolishes extremes of poverty and wealth, exalts work performed in the spirit of service to the rank of worship, recommends the adoption of an auxiliary international language, and provides the necessary agencies for the establishment and safeguarding of a permanent and universal peace. (Shoghi Effendi, in *U.S. Bahá'í News,* No. 85, July 1934, p. 7.)

THE PRINCIPLE OF THE HARMONY OF SCIENCE AND RELIGION

If we say religion is opposed to science, we lack knowledge of either true science or true religion, for both are founded upon the premises and conclusions of reason, and both must bear its test. ('Abdu'l-Bahá, *The Promulgation of Universal Peace,* p. 148.)

Bahá'u'lláh teaches that religion must be in conformity with science and reason. If belief and teaching are opposed to the analysis of reason and principles of science, they are not worthy of acceptance. This principle has not been revealed in any of the former Books of divine teaching. ('Abdu'l-Bahá, *The Promulgation of Universal Peace,* p. 611.)

Between scientists and the followers of religion there has always been controversy and strife for the reason that the latter have proclaimed religion superior in authority to science and considered scientific announcement opposed to the teachings of religion. Bahá'u'lláh declared that religion is in complete harmony with science and reason. If religious belief and doctrine is at variance with reason, it proceeds from the limited mind of man and not from God; therefore, it is unworthy of belief and not deserving of attention; the heart finds no rest in it, and real faith is impossible. How can man believe that which he knows to be opposed to reason? Is this possible? Can the heart accept that which reason denies? Reason is the first faculty of man, and the religion of God is in harmony with it. Bahá'u'lláh has removed this form of dissension and discord from among mankind and reconciled science with religion by revealing the pure teachings of the divine reality. This accomplishment is specialized to Him in this Day. ('Abdu'l-Bahá, *The Promulgation of Universal Peace*, p. 323.)

If religion is opposed to reason and science, faith is impossible; and when faith and confidence in the divine religion are not manifest in the heart, there can be no spiritual attainment. ('Abdu'l-Bahá, *The Promulgation of Universal Peace*, p. 415.)

Religion and Science are intertwined with each other and cannot be separated. These are the two wings with which humanity must fly. One wing is not enough. Every religion which does not concern itself with Science is mere tradition, and that is not the essential. Therefore science, education and civilization are most important necessities for the full religious life. ('Abdu'l-Bahá, *'Abdu'l-Bahá in London*, pp. 28–29.)

God has endowed man with reason that he may perceive what is true. If we insist that such and such a subject is not to be reasoned out and tested according to the established logical modes of the intellect, what is the use of the reason which God has given man? The eye is the organ of sense by which we view the world of outer phenomena; hearing is the faculty for distinguishing sounds; taste senses the properties of objects, such as bitter, sweet; smell detects and differentiates odors; touch reveals attributes of matter and perfects our communication with the outer world; yet after all, the circle and range of perception by the five senses is exceedingly limited. But the intellectual faculty of man is unlimited in its sphere of action. The eye views details perhaps a mile, but the intellect can perceive the far East and West. The ear may hear tone modulations at one thousand feet, but the mind of man can detect the harmonies of the heavenly spheres as they swing in their courses. Mind makes geological discoveries in subterranean depths and determines the processes of creation in the earth's lowest strata. The sciences and arts, all inventions, crafts, trades and their products have come forth from the intellect of man. It is evident that within the human organism the intellect occupies the supreme station. Therefore, if religious belief, principle or creed is not in accordance with the intellect and the power of reason, it is surely superstition. ('Abdu'l-Bahá, *The Promulgation of Universal Peace,* pp. 86–87.)

God has bestowed the gift of mind upon man in order that he may weigh every fact or truth presented to him and adjudge whether it be reasonable. That which conforms to his reason he may accept as true, while that which reason and science cannot sanction may be discarded as imagination and superstition, as a phantom and not reality. ('Abdu'l-Bahá, *The Promulgation of Universal Peace,* p. 528.)

While the religion of God is the promoter of truth, the founder of science and knowledge, it is full of goodwill for learned men; it is the civilizer of mankind, the discoverer of the secrets of nature, and the enlightener of the horizons of the world. Consequently, how can it be said to oppose knowledge? God forbid! Nay, for God, knowledge is the most glorious gift of man and the most noble of human perfections. To oppose knowledge is ignorant, and he who detests knowledge and science is not a man, but rather an animal without intelligence. For knowledge is light, life, felicity, perfection, beauty and the means of approaching the Threshold of Unity. It is the honor and glory of the world of humanity, and the greatest bounty of God. Knowledge is identical with guidance, and ignorance is real error. ('Abdu'l-Bahá, *Some Answered Questions,* p. 137.)

Religion must stand the analysis of reason. It must agree with scientific fact and proof so that science will sanction religion and religion fortify science. Both are indissolubly welded and joined in reality. If statements and teachings of religion are found to be unreasonable and contrary to science, they are outcomes of superstition and imagination. Innumerable doctrines and beliefs of this character have arisen in the past ages. Consider the superstitions and mythology of the Romans, Greeks and Egyptians; all were contrary to religion and science. It is now evident that the beliefs of these nations were superstitions, but in those times they held to them most tenaciously. For example, one of the many Egyptian idols was to those people an authenticated miracle, whereas in reality it was a piece of stone. As science could not sanction the miraculous origin and nature of a piece of rock, the belief in it must have been superstition. It is now evident that it was superstition. Therefore, we must cast aside such beliefs and investigate reality. That which is found to be real and conformable to reason must be accepted, and whatever science and reason cannot support must be rejected as imitation and not reality. Then differences of belief will disappear. All will become as one family, one people, and the same susceptibility to the divine bounty and education will be witnessed among mankind. ('Abdu'l-Bahá, *The Promulgation of Universal Peace*, p. 244.)

How can a man believe to be a fact that which science has proved to be impossible? If he believes in spite of his reason, it is rather ignorant superstition than faith. The true principles of all religions are in conformity with the teachings of science.

The Unity of God is logical, and this idea is not antagonistic to the conclusions arrived at by scientific study.

All religions teach that we must do good, that we must be generous, sincere, truthful, law-abiding, and faithful; all this is reasonable, and logically the only way in which humanity can progress.

All religious laws conform to reason, and are suited to the people for whom they are framed, and for the age in which they are to be obeyed.

Religion has two main parts:

(1) The Spiritual.

(2) The Practical.

The spiritual part never changes. All the Manifestations of God and His Prophets have taught the same truths and given the same spiritual law. They all teach the one code of morality. There is no division in the truth. The Sun has sent forth many rays to illumine human intelligence, the light is always the same.

The practical part of religion deals with exterior forms and ceremonies, and with modes of punishment for certain offences. This is the material side of the law, and guides the customs and manners of the people.

In the time of Moses, there were ten crimes punishable by death. When Christ came this was changed; the old axiom "an eye for an eye, and a tooth for a tooth" was converted into "Love your enemies, do good to them that hate you," the stern old law being changed into one of love, mercy and forbearance!

In the former days the punishment for theft was the cutting off of the right hand; in our time this law could not be so applied. In this age, a man who curses his father is allowed to live, when formerly he would have been put to death. It is therefore evident that whilst the spiritual law never alters, the practical rules must change their application with the necessities of the time. The spiritual aspect of religion is the greater, the more important of the two, and this is the same for all time, it never changes! It is the same, yesterday, today, and forever! "As it was the beginning, is now, and ever shall be."

Now, all questions of morality contained in the spiritual, immutable law of every religion are logically right. If religion were contrary to logical reason then it would cease to be a religion and be merely a tradition. Religion and science are the two wings upon which man's intelligence can soar into the heights, with which the human soul can progress. It is not possible to fly with one wing alone! Should a man try to fly with the wing of religion alone he would quickly fall into the quagmire of superstition, whilst on the other hand, with the wing of science alone he would also make no progress, but fall into the despairing slough of materialism. . . .

. . . I say unto you: weigh carefully in the balance of reason and science everything that is presented to you as religion. If it passes this test, then accept it, for it is truth! If, however, it does not so conform, then reject it, for it is ignorance! . . .

Put all your beliefs into harmony with science; there can be no opposition, for truth is one. When religion, shorn of its superstitions, traditions, and unintelligent dogmas, shows its conformity with science, then will there be a great unifying, cleansing force in the world which will sweep before it all wars, disagreements, discords and struggles—and then will mankind be united in the power of the Love of God. ('Abdu'l-Bahá, *Paris Talks,* no. 44.3–15, 26.)

Bahá'u'lláh has said that learning can be the veil between the soul of man and the eternal truth; in other words, between man and knowledge of God. We have seen that many people who become very advanced in the study of modern physical sciences are led to deny God, and to deny His Prophets. That does not mean that God and the Prophets have not and do not exist. It only means that knowledge has become a veil between their hearts and the light of God. (From a letter written on behalf of Shoghi Effendi, dated 22 April 1954, in *Lights of Guidance,* no. 1822.)

You see our whole approach to each matter is based on the belief that God sends us divinely inspired Educators; what they tell us is fundamentally true, what science tells us today is true; tomorrow may be entirely changed to better explain a new set of facts. (Shoghi Effendi, *Arohanui: Letters to New Zealand,* p. 85.)

Considering that a century ago, nobody knew the nature of matter, and couldn't split any kind of atom, it should not surprise the scientist that 'Abdu'l-Bahá states that copper can be transmuted into gold.

There may come a time, for all we know, when the mass of many atoms can be changed by scientists. We have no way of proving, or disproving at present the statement of 'Abdu'l-Bahá. Just because we cannot demonstrate a contention in the Bahá'í Teachings, does not mean the contention is not true.

The same holds true of the statement of Bahá'u'lláh in the Íqán, regarding transmutation of copper into gold after seventy years, under certain conditions.

We as Bahá'ís must assume that, as He had access to all knowledge, He was referring to a definite physical condition which theoretically might exist. Because we don't know what this condition is in scientific terms, does not refute Bahá'u'lláh's statement at all.

. . . The principle of Faith is to accept anything the Manifestation of God says, once you have accepted Him as being the Manifestation. That is really the crux of the whole matter. It is a question of confidence. (From a letter written on behalf of Shoghi Effendi, dated 14 March 1955, to an individual believer, in *Lights of Guidance,* no. 1580.)

[T]he principle of harmony between religion and science, while it enables us, with the help of reason, to see through the falsity of superstitions, does not imply that truth is limited to what can be explained by current scientific concepts. Not only do all religions have their miracles and mysteries, but religion itself, and certain fundamental religious concepts, such as the nature of the Manifestations of God, are far from being explicable by present-day scientific theories. (The Universal House of Justice, from a letter dated 2 December 1995, to an individual believer.)

Together with the crumbling of barriers separating peoples, our age is witnessing the dissolution of the once insuperable wall that the past assumed would forever separate the life of Heaven from the life of Earth. The scriptures of all religions have always taught the believer to see in service to others not only a moral duty, but an avenue for the soul's own approach to God. Today, the progressive restructuring of society gives this familiar teaching new dimensions of meaning. As the age-old promise of a world animated by principles of justice slowly takes on the character of a realistic goal, meeting the needs of the soul and those of society will increasingly be seen as reciprocal aspects of a mature spiritual life.

If religious leadership is to rise to the challenge that this latter perception represents, such response must begin by acknowledging that religion and science are the two indispensable knowledge systems through which the potentialities of consciousness develop. Far from being in conflict with one another, these fundamental modes of the mind's exploration of reality are mutually dependent and have been most productive in those rare but happy periods of history when their complementary nature has been recognized and they have been able to work together. The insights and skills generated by scientific advance will have always to look to the guidance of spiritual and moral commitment to ensure their appropriate application; religious convictions, no matter how cherished they may be, must submit, willingly and gratefully, to impartial testing by scientific methods. (The Universal House of Justice, *To the World's Religious Leaders*, p. 5.)

Just as there is a fundamental difference between divine Revelation itself and the understanding that believers have of it, so also there is a basic distinction between scientific fact and reasoning on the one hand and the conclusions or theories of scientists on the other. There is, and can be, no conflict between true religion and true science: true religion is revealed by God, while it is through true science that the mind of man "discovers the realities of things and becomes cognizant of their peculiarities and effects, and of the qualities and properties of beings" and "comprehendeth the abstract by the aid of the concrete." However, whenever a statement is made through the lens of human understanding it is thereby limited, for human understanding is limited; and where there is limitation there is the possibility of error; and where there is error, conflicts can arise. For example, at the present time many people are convinced that it is unscientific to believe in God, but, as human enlightenment progresses, the scientists and philosophers of the future will not be, in the words of 'Abdu'l-Bahá, "deniers of the Prophets, ignorant of spiritual susceptibilities, deprived of the heavenly bounties and without belief in the supernatural." (From a letter written on behalf of the Universal House of Justice, dated 26 December 1975, to an individual believer, in *Scholarship,* p. 16.)

The scientific and technological advances occurring in this unusually blessed century portend a great surge forward in the social evolution of the planet, and indicate the means by which the practical problems of humanity may be solved. They provide, indeed, the very means for the administration of the complex life of a united world. Yet barriers persist. Doubts, misconceptions, prejudices, suspicions and narrow self-interest beset nations and peoples in their relations one to another. . . .

If, therefore, humanity has come to a point of paralyzing conflict it must look to itself, to its own negligence, to the siren voices to which it has listened, for the source of the misunderstandings and confusion perpetrated in the name of religion. Those who have held blindly and selfishly to their particular orthodoxies, who have imposed on their votaries erroneous and conflicting interpretations of the pronouncements of the Prophets of God, bear heavy responsibility for this confusion—a confusion compounded by the artificial barriers erected between faith and reason, science and religion. For from a fair-minded examination of the actual utterances of the Founders of the great religions, and of the social milieus in which they were obliged to carry out their missions, there is nothing to support the contentions and prejudices deranging the religious communities of mankind and therefore all human affairs. (The Universal House of Justice, *The Promise of World Peace,* p. 1.)

Chapter Two

THE ACQUISITION OF
THE SCIENCES

VALUE OF SCIENTIFIC KNOWLEDGE

Praise and thanksgiving be unto Providence that out of all the realities in existence He has chosen the reality of man and has honored it with intellect and wisdom, the two most luminous lights in either world. . . .

This supreme emblem of God stands first in the order of creation and first in rank, taking precedence over all created things. Witness to it is the Holy Tradition, "Before all else, God created the mind." From the dawn of creation, it was made to be revealed in the temple of man. ('Abdu'l-Bahá, *The Secret of Divine Civilization,* ¶1, 2.)

Arts, crafts and sciences uplift the world of being, and are conducive to its exaltation. Knowledge is as wings to man's life, and a ladder for his ascent. Its acquisition is incumbent upon everyone. The knowledge of such sciences, however, should be acquired as can profit the peoples of the earth, and not those which begin with words and end with words. Great indeed is the claim of scientists and craftsmen on the peoples of the world. . . .

In truth, knowledge is a veritable treasure for man, and a source of glory, of bounty, of joy, of exaltation, of cheer and gladness unto him. (Bahá'u'lláh, *Epistle to the Son of the Wolf,* pp. 26–27.)

Verily We love those men of knowledge who have brought to light such things as promote the best interests of humanity, and We aided them through the potency of Our behest, for well are We able to achieve Our purpose. (Bahá'u'lláh, *Tablets of Bahá'u'lláh,* p. 150.)

Consider Hippocrates, the physician. He was one of the eminent philosophers who believed in God and acknowledged His sovereignty. After him came Socrates who was indeed wise, accomplished and righteous. He practiced self-denial, repressed his appetites for selfish desires and turned away from material pleasures. He withdrew to the mountains where he dwelt in a cave. He dissuaded men from worshipping idols and taught them the way of God, the Lord of Mercy, until the ignorant rose up against him. They arrested him and put him to death in prison. Thus relateth to thee this swift-moving Pen. What a penetrating vision into philosophy this eminent man had! He is the most distinguished of all philosophers and was highly versed in wisdom. We testify that he is one of the heroes in this field and an outstanding champion dedicated unto it. He had a profound knowledge of such sciences as were current amongst men as well as of those which were veiled from their minds. Methinks he drank one draught when the Most Great Ocean overflowed with gleaming and life-giving waters. He it is who perceived a unique, a tempered, and a pervasive nature in things, bearing the closest likeness to the human spirit, and he discovered this nature to be distinct from the substance of things in their refined form. He hath a special pronouncement on this weighty theme. Wert thou to ask from the worldly wise of this generation about this exposition, thou wouldst witness their incapacity to grasp it. Verily, thy Lord speaketh the truth but most people comprehend not.

After Socrates came the divine Plato who was a pupil of the former and occupied the chair of philosophy as his successor. He acknowledged his belief in God and in His signs which pervade all that hath been and shall be. Then came Aristotle, the well-known man of knowledge. He it is who discovered the power of gaseous matter. These men who stand out as leaders of the people and are pre-eminent among them, one and all acknowledged their belief in the immortal Being Who holdeth in His grasp the reins of all sciences. (Bahá'u'lláh, *Tablets of Bahá'u'lláh,* p. 146.)

God made religion and science to be the measure, as it were, of our understanding. Take heed that you neglect not such a wonderful power. Weigh all things in this balance. ('Abdu'l-Bahá, *Paris Talks,* no. 44.24.)

Would the extension of education, the development of useful arts and sciences, the promotion of industry and technology, be harmful things? For such endeavor lifts the individual within the mass and raises him out of the depths of ignorance to the highest reaches of knowledge and human excellence. ('Abdu'l-Bahá, *The Secret of Divine Civilization,* ¶25.)

Scientific knowledge is the highest attainment upon the human plane, for science is the discoverer of realities. It is of two kinds: material and spiritual. Material science is the investigation of natural phenomena; divine science is the discovery and realization of spiritual verities. The world of humanity must acquire both. A bird has two wings; it cannot fly with one. Material and spiritual science are the two wings of human uplift and attainment. Both are necessary—one the natural, the other supernatural; one material, the other divine. By the divine we mean the discovery of the mysteries of God, the comprehension of spiritual realities, the wisdom of God, inner significances of the heavenly religions and foundation of the law. ('Abdu'l-Bahá, *The Promulgation of Universal Peace,* pp. 195–96.)

For if a learned individual has no knowledge of the sacred Scriptures and the entire field of divine and natural science, of religious jurisprudence and the arts of government and the varied learning of the time and the great events of history, he might prove unequal to an emergency, and this is inconsistent with the necessary qualification of comprehensive knowledge. ('Abdu'l-Bahá, *The Secret of Divine Civilization,* ¶64.)

If we look with a perceiving eye upon the world of creation, we find that all existing things may be classified as follows: first, mineral—that is to say, matter or substance appearing in various forms of composition; second, vegetable—possessing the virtues of the mineral plus the power of augmentation or growth, indicating a degree higher and more specialized than the mineral; third, animal—possessing the attributes of the mineral and vegetable plus the power of sense perception; fourth, human—the highest specialized organism of visible creation, embodying the qualities of the mineral, vegetable and animal plus an ideal endowment absolutely absent in the lower kingdoms—the power of intellectual investigation into the mysteries of outer phenomena. The outcome of this intellectual endowment is science, which is especially characteristic of man. This scientific power investigates and apprehends created objects and the laws surrounding them. It is the discoverer of the hidden and mysterious secrets of the material universe and is peculiar to man alone. The most noble and praiseworthy accomplishment of man, therefore, is scientific knowledge and attainment. ('Abdu'l-Bahá, *The Promulgation of Universal Peace,* pp. 39–40.)

For all created things except man are subjects or captives of nature; they cannot deviate in the slightest degree from nature's law and control. . . .

According to the limitations of his physical powers man was intended by creation to live upon the earth, but through the exercise of his mental faculties, he removes the restriction of this law. . . . All the sciences and arts we now enjoy and utilize were once mysteries, and according to the mandates of nature should have remained hidden and latent, but the human intellect has broken through the laws surrounding them and discovered the underlying realities. The mind of man has taken these mysteries out of the plane of invisibility and brought them into the plane of the known and visible.

In nature there is the law of the survival of the fittest. Even if man be not educated, then according to the natural institutes this natural law will demand of man supremacy. The purpose and object of schools, colleges and universities is to educate man and thereby rescue and redeem him from the exigencies and defects of nature and to awaken within him the capability of controlling and appropriating nature's bounties. . . .

. . . [I]t is not intended that the world of humanity should be left to its natural state. It is in need of the education divinely provided for it. ('Abdu'l-Bahá, *The Promulgation of Universal Peace,* pp. 496–97, 499.)

The virtues of humanity are many, but science is the most noble of them all. The distinction which man enjoys above and beyond the station of the animal is due to this paramount virtue. It is a bestowal of God; it is not material; it is divine. Science is an effulgence of the Sun of Reality, the power of investigating and discovering the verities of the universe, the means by which man finds a pathway to God. All the powers and attributes of man are human and hereditary in origin—outcomes of nature's processes—except the intellect, which is supernatural. Through intellectual and intelligent inquiry science is the discoverer of all things. It unites present and past, reveals the history of bygone nations and events, and confers upon man today the essence of all human knowledge and attainment throughout the ages. By intellectual processes and logical deductions of reason this superpower in man can penetrate the mysteries of the future and anticipate its happenings.

Science is the first emanation from God toward man. All created beings embody the potentiality of material perfection, but the power of intellectual investigation and scientific acquisition is a higher virtue specialized to man alone. Other beings and organisms are deprived of this potentiality and attainment. God has created or deposited this love of reality in man. The development and progress of a nation is according to the measure and degree of that nation's scientific attainments. Through this means its greatness is continually increased, and day by day the welfare and prosperity of its people are assured.

All blessings are divine in origin, but none can be compared with this power of intellectual investigation and research, which is an eternal gift producing fruits of unending delight. Man is ever partaking of these fruits. All other blessings are temporary; this is an everlasting possession. Even sovereignty has its limitations and overthrow; this is a kingship and dominion which none may usurp or destroy. Briefly, it is an eternal blessing and divine bestowal, the supreme gift of

God to man. Therefore, you should put forward your most earnest efforts toward the acquisition of science and arts. The greater your attainment, the higher your standard in the divine purpose. The man of science is perceiving and endowed with vision, whereas he who is ignorant and neglectful of this development is blind. The investigating mind is attentive, alive; the callous and indifferent mind is deaf and dead. A scientific man is a true index and representative of humanity, for through processes of inductive reasoning and research he is informed of all that appertains to humanity, its status, conditions and happenings. He studies the human body politic, understands social problems and weaves the web and texture of civilization. In fact, science may be likened to a mirror wherein the infinite forms and images of existing things are revealed and reflected. It is the very foundation of all individual and national development. Without this basis of investigation, development is impossible. Therefore, seek with diligent endeavor the knowledge and attainment of all that lies within the power of this wonderful bestowal.

We have already stated that science or the attribute of scientific penetration is supernatural and that all other blessings of God are within the boundary of nature. What is the proof of this? All created things except man are captives of nature. The stars and suns swinging through infinite space, all earthly forms of life and existence—whether mineral, vegetable or animal—come under the dominion and control of natural law. Man through scientific knowledge and power rules nature and utilizes her laws to do his bidding. According to natural limitations he is a creature of earth, restricted to life upon its surface, but through scientific utilization of material laws he soars in the sky, sails upon the ocean and dives beneath it. The products of his invention and discovery, so familiar to us in daily life, were once mysteries of nature. For instance, man has brought electricity out of the plane of the invisible into the plane of the visible, harnessed and imprisoned that mysterious natural agent and made it the servant of his needs and wishes. Similar instances are many, but we will not prolong this. Man, as it were, takes the sword out of nature's hand and with it for his scepter of authority dominates nature itself. Nature is without the crown of human faculties and attributes. Man possesses conscious intelligence and reflection; nature does not. This is an established fundamental among philosophers. Man is endowed with volition and memory; nature has neither. Man can seek out the mysteries latent in nature, whereas nature is not conscious of her own hidden phenomena. Man is progressive; nature is stationary, without the power of progression or retrogression. Man is endowed with ideal virtues—for example, intellection, volition, faith, confession and acknowledgment of God—while nature is devoid of all these. The ideal faculties of man, including the capacity for scientific acquisition, are beyond nature's ken. These are powers whereby man is differentiated and distinguished from all other forms of life. This is the bestowal of divine idealism, the crown adorning human heads. Notwithstanding the gift of this supernatural power, it is most amazing that materialists still consider themselves within the bonds and captivity of nature. The truth is that God has endowed man with virtues, powers and ideal faculties of which nature is entirely bereft and by which man is elevated, distinguished and superior. We must thank God for these bestowals, for these powers He has given us, for this crown He has placed upon our heads.

How shall we utilize these gifts and expend these bounties? By directing our efforts toward the unification of the human race. We must use these powers in establishing the oneness of the world of humanity, appreciate these virtues by accomplishing the unity of whites and blacks, devote this divine intelligence to the perfecting of amity and accord among all branches of the human family so that under the protection and providence of God the East and West may hold each other's hands and become as lovers. Then will mankind be as one nation, one race and kind—as waves of one ocean. ('Abdu'l-Bahá, *The Promulgation of Universal Peace*, pp. 66–70.)

The world will be filled with science, with the knowledge of the reality of the mysteries of beings, and with the knowledge of God.

Now consider, in this great century which is the cycle of Bahá'u'lláh, what progress science and knowledge have made, how many secrets of existence have been discovered, how many great inventions have been brought to light and are day by day multiplying in number. Before long, material science and learning, as well as the knowledge of God, will make such progress and will show forth such wonders that the beholders will be amazed. Then the mystery of this verse in Isaiah, "For the earth shall be full of the knowledge of the Lord," will be completely evident. ('Abdu'l-Bahá, *Some Answered Questions,* p. 64.)

PROCESS FOR EFFECTIVE STUDY

The source of crafts, sciences and arts is the power of reflection. Make ye every effort that out of this ideal mine there may gleam forth such pearls of wisdom and utterance as will promote the well-being and harmony of all the kindreds of the earth. (Bahá'u'lláh, *Tablets of Bahá'u'lláh,* p. 72.)

Look at the world and ponder a while upon it. It unveileth the book of its own self before thine eyes and revealeth that which the Pen of thy Lord, the Fashioner, the All-Informed, hath inscribed therein. It will acquaint thee with that which is within it and upon it and will give thee such clear explanations as to make thee independent of every eloquent expounder. (Bahá'u'lláh, *Tablets of Bahá'u'lláh,* pp. 141–42.)

Bahá'u'lláh says there is a sign (from God) in every phenomenon: the sign of the intellect is contemplation and the sign of contemplation is silence, because it is impossible for a man to do two things at one time—he cannot both speak and meditate.

It is an axiomatic fact that while you meditate you are speaking with your own spirit. In that state of mind you put certain questions to your spirit and the spirit answers: the light breaks forth and the reality is revealed.

You cannot apply the name "man" to any being void of this faculty of meditation; without it he would be a mere animal, lower than the beasts.

Through the faculty of meditation man attains to eternal life; through it he receives the breath of the Holy Spirit—the bestowal of the Spirit is given in reflection and meditation.

The spirit of man is itself informed and strengthened during meditation; through it affairs of which man knew nothing are unfolded before his view. Through it he receives Divine inspiration, through it he receives heavenly food.

Meditation is the key for opening the doors of mysteries. In that state man abstracts himself: in that state man withdraws himself from all outside objects; in that subjective mood he is immersed in the ocean of spiritual life and can unfold the secrets of things-in-themselves. To illustrate this, think of man as endowed with two kinds of sight; when the power of insight is being used the outward power of vision does not see.

This faculty of meditation frees man from the animal nature, discerns the reality of things, puts man in touch with God.

This faculty brings forth from the invisible plane the sciences and arts. Through the meditative faculty inventions are made possible, colossal undertakings are carried out; through it governments can run smoothly. Through this faculty man enters into the very Kingdom of God. ('Abdu'l-Bahá, *Paris Talks,* no. 54.8–15.)

So long as the thoughts of an individual are scattered he will achieve no results, but if his thinking be concentrated on a single point wonderful will be the fruits thereof.

One cannot obtain the full force of the sunlight when it is cast on a flat mirror, but once the sun shineth upon a concave mirror, or on a lens that is convex, all its heat will be concentrated on a single point, and that one point will burn the hottest. Thus is it necessary to focus one's thinking on a single point so that it will become an effective force. ('Abdu'l-Bahá, *Selections from the Writings of 'Abdu'l-Bahá,* no. 73.1–2.)

Thou didst write as to the question of spiritual discoveries. The spirit of man is a circumambient power that encompasseth the realities of all things. Whatsoever thou dost see about thee—wondrous products of human workmanship, inventions, discoveries and like evidences—each one of these was once a secret hidden away in the realm of the unknown. The human spirit laid that secret bare, and drew it forth from the unseen into the visible world. There is, for example,

the power of steam, and photography and the pho-
nograph, and wireless telegraphy, and advances in
mathematics: each and every one of these was once a
mystery, a closely guarded secret, yet the human spirit
unraveled these secrets and brought them out of the
invisible into the light of day. Thus is it clear that the
human spirit is an all-encompassing power that exer-
teth its dominion over the inner essences of all created
things, uncovering the well kept mysteries of the phenomenal world.

The divine spirit, however, doth unveil divine realities and universal mysteries that lie within the spiritual
world. It is my hope that thou wilt attain unto this divine spirit, so that thou mayest uncover the secrets of
the other world, as well as the mysteries of the world
below. ('Abdu'l-Bahá, *Selections from the Writings of
'Abdu'l-Bahá*, no. 145.1–2.)

There are only four accepted methods of comprehension—that is to say, the realities of things are understood by these four methods.

The first method is by the senses—that is to say,
all that the eye, the ear, the taste, the smell, the touch
perceive is understood by this method. Today this
method is considered the most perfect by all the European philosophers: they say that the principal method
of gaining knowledge is through the senses; they consider it supreme, although it is imperfect, for it com-
mits errors. For example, the greatest of the senses is
the power of sight. The sight sees the mirage as water,

and it sees images reflected in mirrors as real and existent; large bodies which are distant appear to be small, and a whirling point appears as a circle. The sight believes the earth to be motionless and sees the sun in motion, and in many similar cases it makes mistakes. Therefore, we cannot trust it.

The second is the method of reason, which was that of the ancient philosophers, the pillars of wisdom; this is the method of the understanding. They proved things by reason and held firmly to logical proofs; all their arguments are arguments of reason. Notwithstanding this, they differed greatly, and their opinions were contradictory. They even changed their views—that is to say, during twenty years they would prove the existence of a thing by logical arguments, and afterward they would deny it by logical arguments—so much so that Plato at first logically proved the immobility of the earth and the movement of the sun; later by logical arguments he proved that the sun was the stationary center, and that the earth was moving. Afterward the Ptolemaic theory was spread abroad, and the idea of Plato was entirely forgotten, until at last a new observer again called it to life. Thus all the mathematicians disagreed, although they relied upon arguments of reason. In the same way, by logical arguments, they would prove a problem at a certain time, then afterward by arguments of the same nature they would deny it. So one of the philosophers would firmly uphold a theory for a time with strong arguments and proofs to support it, which afterward he would retract and contradict by arguments of reason. Therefore, it is evident that the method of reason is not perfect, for the differences of the ancient philosophers, the want of stability and the variations of their opinions, prove this. For if it were perfect, all ought to be united in their ideas and agreed in their opinions.

The third method of understanding is by tradition—that is, through the text of the Holy Scriptures—for people say, "In the Old and New Testaments, God spoke thus." This method equally is not perfect, because the traditions are understood by the reason. As the reason itself is liable to err, how can it be said that in interpreting the meaning of the traditions it will not err, for it is possible for it to make mistakes, and certainty cannot be attained. This is the method of the religious leaders; whatever they understand and comprehend from the text of the books is that which their reason understands from the text, and not necessarily the real truth; for the reason is like a balance, and the meanings contained in the text of the Holy Books are like the thing which is weighed. If the balance is untrue, how can the weight be ascertained?

Know then: that which is in the hands of people, that which they believe, is liable to error. For, in proving or disproving a thing, if a proof is brought forward which is taken from the evidence of our senses, this method, as has become evident, is not perfect; if the proofs are intellectual, the same is true; or if they are traditional, such proofs also are not perfect. Therefore, there is no standard in the hands of people upon which we can rely.

But the bounty of the Holy Spirit gives the true method of comprehension which is infallible and indubitable. This is through the help of the Holy Spirit which comes to man, and this is the condition in which certainty can alone be attained. ('Abdu'l-Bahá, *Some Answered Questions,* pp. 296–99.)

We are living in a day of reliance upon material conditions. Men imagine that the great size and strength of a ship, the perfection of machinery or the skill of a navigator will ensure safety, but these disasters sometimes take place that men may know that God is the real Protector. . . .

Let no one imagine that these words imply that man should not be thorough and careful in his undertakings. God has endowed man with intelligence so that he may safeguard and protect himself. Therefore, he must provide and surround himself with all that scientific skill can produce. He must be deliberate, thoughtful and thorough in his purposes, build the best ship and provide the most experienced captain; yet, withal, let him rely upon God and consider God as the one Keeper. If God protects, nothing can imperil man's safety; and if it be not His will to safeguard, no amount of preparation and precaution will avail. ('Abdu'l-Bahá, *The Promulgation of Universal Peace,* pp. 65–66.)

Among those matters which require thorough revision and reform is the method of studying the various branches of knowledge and the organization of the academic curriculum. From lack of organization, education has become haphazard and confused. Trifling subjects which should not call for elaboration receive undue attention, to such an extent that students, over long periods of time, waste their minds and their energies on material that is pure supposition, in no way susceptible of proof, such study consisting in going deep into statements and concepts which careful examination would establish as not even unlikely, but rather as unalloyed superstition, and representing the investigation of useless conceits and the chasing of absurdities. There can be no doubt that to concern oneself with such illusions, to examine into and lengthily debate such idle propositions, is nothing but a waste of time and a marring of the days of one's life. Not only this, but it also prevents the individual from undertaking the study of those arts and sciences of which society stands in dire need. The individual should, prior to engaging in the study of any subject, ask himself what its uses are and what fruit and result will derive from it. If it is a useful branch of knowledge, that is, if society will gain important benefits from it, then he should certainly pursue it with all his heart. ('Abdu'l-Bahá, *The Secret of Divine Civilization,* ¶187.)

We need very much the sound, sane, element of thinking which a scientifically trained mind has to offer. When such intellectual powers are linked to deep faith a tremendous teaching potential is created. (From a letter written on behalf of Shoghi Effendi, quoted in a letter written on behalf of the Universal House of Justice, dated 19 October 1993, to an individual believer, in *Scholarship,* p. 18.)

It is hoped that all the Bahá'í students will . . . be led to investigate and analyse the principles of the Faith and to correlate them with the modern aspects of philosophy and science. Every intelligent and thoughtful young Bahá'í should always approach the Cause in this way, for therein lies the very essence of the principle of independent investigation of truth. (From a letter written on behalf of Shoghi Effendi, dated 6 August 1933, to an individual believer, in *Scholarship,* p. 17.)

You are already a qualified practitioner in your field, and no doubt you give advice on the basis of what you have learned from study and experience—a whole fabric of concepts about the human mind, its growth, development and proper functioning, which you have learned and evolved without reference to the teachings of Bahá'u'lláh. Now, as a Bahá'í, you know that what Bahá'u'lláh teaches about the purpose of human life, the nature of the human being and the proper conduct of human lives, is divinely revealed and therefore true. However, it will inevitably take time for you not only to study the Bahá'í teachings so that you clearly understand them, but also to work out how they modify your professional concepts. This is, of course, not an unusual predicament for a scientist. How often in the course of research is a factor discovered which requires a revolution in thinking over a wide field of human endeavour. You must be guided in each case by your own professional knowledge and judgement as illuminated by your growing knowledge of the Bahá'í teachings; undoubtedly you will find that your own understanding of the human problems dealt with in your work will change and develop and you will see new and improved ways of helping the people who come to you.

Psychology is still a very young and inexact science, and as the years go by Bahá'í psychologists, who know from the teachings of Bahá'u'lláh the true pattern of human life, will be able to make great strides in the development of this science, and will help profoundly in the alleviation of human suffering. (The Universal House of Justice, from a letter dated 6 February 1973, *Messages from the Universal House of Justice, 1963–1986,* no. 126.10.)

With regard to the harmony of science and religion, the Writings of the Central Figures and the commentaries of the Guardian make abundantly clear that the task of humanity, including the Bahá'í community . . . is to create a global civilization which embodies both the spiritual and material dimensions of existence. The nature and scope of such a civilization are still beyond anything the present generation can conceive. The prosecution of this vast enterprise will depend on a progressive interaction between the truths and principles of religion and the discoveries and insights of scientific inquiry. This entails living with ambiguities as a natural and inescapable feature of the process of exploring reality. It also requires us not to limit science to any particular school of thought or methodological approach postulated in the course of its development. (From a letter written on behalf of the Universal House of Justice, dated 19 May 1995, to an individual believer, in *Science and Religion,* p. 1.)

FIELDS OF STUDY

It is permissible to study sciences and arts, but such sciences as are useful and would redound to the progress and advancement of the people. Thus hath it been decreed by Him Who is the Ordainer, the All-Wise. (Bahá'u'lláh, *Tablets of Bahá'u'lláh,* p. 25.)

Such arts and sciences, however, as are productive of good results, and bring forth their fruit, and are conducive to the well-being and tranquility of men have been, and will remain, acceptable before God. (Bahá'u'lláh, *Epistle to the Son of the Wolf,* p. 19.)

We have permitted you to read such sciences as are profitable unto you, not such as end in idle disputation; better is this for you, if ye be of them that comprehend. (Bahá'u'lláh, The Kitáb-i-Aqdas, ¶77.)

Fruitless sciences is what Bahá'u'lláh, refers to, like metaphysical hair splittings, and other abstract things carried to the extreme. (From a letter written on behalf of Shoghi Effendi, dated 30 July 1956, to an individual believer, in *Lights of Guidance,* no. 1749.)

At the outset of every endeavor, it is incumbent to look to the end of it. Of all the arts and sciences, set the children to studying those which will result in advantage to man, will ensure his progress and elevate his rank. Thus the noisome odors of lawlessness will be dispelled, and thus through the high endeavors of the nation's leaders, all will live cradled, secure and in peace.

The Great Being saith: The learned of the day must direct the people to acquire those branches of knowledge which are of use, that both the learned themselves and the generality of mankind may derive benefits therefrom. Such academic pursuits as begin and end in words alone have never been and will never be of any worth. (Bahá'u'lláh, *Tablets of Bahá'u'lláh,* pp. 168–69.)

Among other teachings and principles Bahá'u'lláh counsels the education of all members of society. No individual should be denied or deprived of intellectual training, although each should receive according to capacity. None must be left in the grades of ignorance, for ignorance is a defect in the human world. All mankind must be given a knowledge of science and philosophy—that is, as much as may be deemed necessary. All cannot be scientists and philosophers, but each should be educated according to his needs and deserts. ('Abdu'l-Bahá, *The Promulgation of Universal Peace*, p. 150.)

But education is of three kinds: material, human and spiritual. Material education is concerned with the progress and development of the body, through gaining its sustenance, its material comfort and ease. This education is common to animals and man.

Human education signifies civilization and progress—that is to say, government, administration, charitable works, trades, arts and handicrafts, sciences, great inventions and discoveries and elaborate institutions, which are the activities essential to man as distinguished from the animal.

Divine education is that of the Kingdom of God: it consists in acquiring divine perfections, and this is true education; for in this state man becomes the focus of divine blessings, the manifestation of the words, "Let Us make man in Our image, and after Our likeness." This is the goal of the world of humanity. ('Abdu'l-Bahá, *Some Answered Questions*, p. 7.)

And among the teachings of Bahá'u'lláh is the promotion of education. Every child must be instructed in sciences as much as is necessary. If the parents are able to provide the expenses of this education, it is well, otherwise the community must provide the means for the teaching of that child. ('Abdu'l-Bahá, *Selections from the Writings of 'Abdu'l-Bahá*, no. 227.23.)

Every child, without exception, must from his earliest years make a thorough study of the art of reading and writing, and according to his own tastes and inclinations and the degree of his capacity and powers, devote extreme diligence to the acquisition of learning beneficial arts and skills, various languages, speech, and contemporary technology. (Shoghi Effendi, from a letter dated 8 June 1925, to the National Spiritual Assembly of Persia, in *Science and Religion,* p. 2.)

Study the sciences, acquire more and more knowledge. Assuredly one may learn to the end of one's life! Use your knowledge always for the benefit of others; so may war cease on the face of this beautiful earth, and a glorious edifice of peace and concord be raised. ('Abdu'l-Bahá, *Paris Talks,* no. 11.13.)

Thou shouldst endeavour to study the science of medicine. It is extremely useful and serveth as the greatest instrument for the dissemination of the Cause. It is absolutely imperative that thou acquire this bounty. Strive day and night that thou mayest become highly qualified in this science. And when thou wishest to dispense treatment set thy heart toward the Abhá Kingdom,* entreating Divine confirmations. ('Abdu'l-Bahá, in *Lights of Guidance,* no. 961.)

---

* *The Most Glorious Kingdom;* The spiritual world beyond this one.

Strive as much as possible to become proficient in the science of agriculture, for in accordance with the divine teachings the acquisition of sciences and the perfection of arts are considered acts of worship. If a man engageth with all his power in the acquisition of a science or in the perfection of an art, it is as if he has been worshipping God in churches and temples. Thus as thou enterest a school of agriculture and strivest in the acquisition of that science thou art day and night engaged in acts of worship—acts that are accepted at the threshold of the Almighty. What bounty greater than this that science should be considered as an act of worship and art as service to the Kingdom of God. ('Abdu'l-Bahá, *Selections from the Writings of 'Abdu'l-Bahá*, no. 126.1.)

Woman must especially devote her energies and abilities toward the industrial and agricultural sciences, seeking to assist mankind in that which is most needful. By this means she will demonstrate capability and ensure recognition of equality in the social and economic equation. ('Abdu'l-Bahá, *The Promulgation of Universal Peace*, p. 395.)

Great emphasis is placed on education in the Bahá'í Faith as a means of promoting the advancement of women. The religion not only upholds the principle of universal education, but it accords priority to the education of girls and women when resources are limited, since it is only through educated mothers that the benefits of knowledge can be most effectively and rapidly diffused throughout society. It advocates that girls and boys follow the same curriculum in school, and women are encouraged to study the arts, crafts, sciences and professions and to enter all fields of work, even those traditionally the exclusive province of men. (Bahá'í International Community, "Religion as an Agent for Promoting the Advancement of Women at All Levels.")

Bahá'u'lláh states that "Special regard must be paid to agriculture." He characterizes it as an activity which is "conducive to the advancement of mankind and to the reconstruction of the world," 'Abdu'l-Bahá asserts that the fundamental basis of the community is agriculture,—tillage of the soil. . . .

He describes agriculture as "a noble science" whose practice is an "act of worship," and He encourages both women and men to engage in "agricultural sciences." He indicates that should an individual "become proficient in this field, he will become a means of providing for the comfort of untold numbers of people." (The Research Department of the Universal House of Justice, in *The Compilation of Compilations, vol. I,* p. 81.)

The friends should be encouraged not to waste time on such things as astrology, etc., which you mention. They cannot be forbidden to do so. The exercise of our free will to choose to do the right things is much

more important. (From a letter written on behalf of
Shoghi Effendi, dated 30 July 1956, to an individual
believer, in *Lights of Guidance,* no. 1749.)

In response to your letter of . . . in which you seek
guidance on the question of chosen professions vis-
a-vis the statement of Bahá'u'lláh concerning sciences
which begin in words and end in mere words and the
pursuit of study in pure mathematics and the classics,
the Universal House of Justice has instructed us to
share with you an excerpt from a letter to an individual believer written in 1947 on behalf of the beloved
Guardian: Philosophy, as you will study it and later
teach it, is certainly not one of the sciences that begins
and ends in words. Fruitless excursions into metaphysical hair-splittings is meant, not a sound branch of
learning like philosophy.

In these words the Guardian has enunciated the
general principle. Turning to the specific instance of
the science of pure mathematics, the reference in the
Eleventh Glad Tidings . . . regarding such sciences as
are profitable, which lead and conduce to the eleva-
tion of mankind, must be placed in the context of
the meaning of sciences as employed by the Manifestation. Bahá'u'lláh's comment about sciences which
begin and end in mere words does not apply to the
systematic study of natural phenomena in order to
discover the laws of order in the physical universe, an
order which mathematics seeks to explore. Pure mathematics frequently has application in practical mat-

ters, such as, for example, group theory or the study of fundamental particles. (From a letter written on behalf of the Universal House of Justice, dated 24 May 1988, to an individual believer, in *Scholarship,* p. 19.)

In the study of the Revelation of God, an individual's proficiency in one of the physical or social sciences, in law, philology, or other fields of specialization will often throw valuable light on issues being examined, and such contributions are greatly to be appreciated. (Extracts from letters sent on behalf of the Universal House of Justice to individual believers concerning scholarship and related subjects, prepared 20 July 1997.)

The opportunity which electronic communication technology provides for more speedy and thorough consultation among the friends is highly significant. Without doubt, it represents another manifestation of a development eagerly anticipated by the Guardian when he foresaw the creation of "a mechanism of world intercommunication . . . embracing the whole planet, freed from national hindrances and restrictions, and functioning with marvellous swiftness and perfect regularity."

As you well appreciate, the extent to which such technology advances the work of the Faith depends, of course, on the manner in which it is used. As a medium for Bahá'ís to exchange views, it imposes on participants the same requirements of moderation, candour, and courtesy as would be the case in any other discussion. Likewise, those involved should avoid belittling the views of one another. In this regard, the House of Justice has noted your understandable repugnance at an apparent temptation to use misleading and invidious labels like "traditionalists" and "liberals," which divide the Bahá'í community. To the extent that this divisive habit of mind may persist in the Bahá'í community, it is obviously a carry-over from non-Bahá'í society and a manifestation of an immature conception of life. If Bahá'ís were to persist in this mode of thinking, it would bring to naught even the most worthwhile intellectual endeavour, as has so conspicuously been the case with societies of the past.

Most important of all, as with any exploration by Bahá'ís of the beliefs and practices of their Faith, electronic discussion will serve the interests of the Cause and its members only as it is conducted within the framework of the Bahá'í Teachings and the truths they enshrine. To attempt to discuss the Cause of God apart from or with disdain for the authoritative guidance inherent in these Teachings would clearly be a logical contradiction. To take the first point mentioned in your letter, it is obvious that seeking to impose limits on the universality of the authority of God's Manifestation would lead to the frustration of serious scholarly work and generate disharmony within an effort whose success depends precisely upon a spirit of unity and mutual trust. (From a letter written on behalf of the Universal House of Justice, dated 19 May 1995, in *Issues Related to the Study of the Bahá'í Faith,* pp. 17–18.)

Since you have raised the question of whether physics is more than tangentially related to Bahá'í issues, you might consider the following comments of a well-known scientific thinker, who is not a Bahá'í, about the correlation between the Bahá'í Teachings and recent developments in the physical sciences:

"In our times we can only survive, and our civilization can only flower, if we reorient the conventional wisdom and achieve the new insights which have been proclaimed by the Bahá'í Faith and which are now also supported by the latest discoveries of the empirical sciences."

"Bahá'ís proclaim that the most important condition that can bring about peace is unity—the unity of families, of nations, and of the great currents of thought and inquiry that we denote science and religion. Maturity, in turn, is a prerequisite for such unity. This is evolutionary thinking, and its validity is shown by the new theories which emerge from nonequilibrium thermodynamics, dynamical systems theory, cybernetics, and the related sciences of complexity. They are supported by detailed empirical investigations in such fields as physical cosmology, paleobiological macroevolutionary theory, and new trends in historiography." (From a letter written on behalf of the Universal House of Justice, dated 19 October 1993, in *Issues Related to the Study of the Bahá'í Faith,* p. 16.)

Chapter Three

THE LAWS:
NATURAL AND SPIRITUAL

ONE UNIVERSAL LAW
CONNECTING ALL THINGS

The organization of God is one; the evolution of existence is one; the divine system is one. Whether they be small or great beings, all are subject to one law and system. ('Abdu'l-Bahá, *Some Answered Questions,* p. 198.)

It is obvious that all created things are connected one to another by a linkage complete and perfect, even, for example, as are the members of the human body. Note how all the members and component parts of the human body are connected one to another. In the same way, all the members of this endless universe are linked one to another. The foot and the step, for example, are connected to the ear and the eye; the eye must look ahead before the step is taken. The ear must hear before the eye will carefully observe. And whatever member of the human body is deficient, produceth a deficiency in the other members. The brain is connected with the heart and stomach, the lungs are connected with all the members. So is it with the other members of the body.

And each one of these members hath its own special function. The mind force—whether we call it preexistent or contingent—doth direct and coordinate all the members of the human body, seeing to it that each part or member duly performeth its own special function. If, however, there be some interruption in the power of the mind, all the members will fail to carry out their essential functions, deficiencies will appear in the body and the functioning of its members, and the power will prove ineffective.

Likewise, look into this endless universe: a universal power inevitably existeth, which encompasseth all, directing and regulating all the parts of this infinite creation; and were it not for this Director, this Coordinator, the universe would be flawed and deficient. It would be even as a madman; whereas ye can see that this endless creation carrieth out its functions in perfect order, every separate part of it performing its own task with complete reliability, nor is there any flaw to be found in all its workings. Thus it is clear that a Universal Power existeth, directing and regulating this infinite universe. Every rational mind can grasp this fact. ('Abdu'l-Bahá, *Selections from the Writings of 'Abdu'l-Bahá,* no. 21.6–8.)

Universal beings resemble and can be compared to particular beings, for both are subjected to one natural system, one universal law and divine organization. So you will find the smallest atoms in the universal system are similar to the greatest beings of the universe. It is clear that they come into existence from one laboratory of might under one natural system and one universal law; therefore, they may be compared to one another. ('Abdu'l-Bahá, *Some Answered Questions,* p. 182.)

[A]ll these endless beings which inhabit the world, whether man, animal, vegetable, mineral—whatever they may be—are surely, each one of them, composed of elements. There is no doubt that this perfection which is in all beings is caused by the creation of God from the composing elements, by their appropriate mingling and proportionate quantities, the mode of their composition, and the influence of other beings. For all beings are connected together like a chain; and reciprocal help, assistance and interaction belonging to the properties of things are the causes of the existence, development and growth of created beings. It is confirmed through evidences and proofs that every being universally acts upon other beings, either absolutely or through association. ('Abdu'l-Bahá, *Some Answered Questions,* p. 178.)

When we carefully investigate the kingdoms of existence and observe the phenomena of the universe about us, we discover the absolute order and perfection of creation. The dull minerals in their affinities, plants and vegetables with power of growth, animals in their instinct, man with conscious intellect and the heavenly orbs moving obediently through limitless space are all found subject to universal law, most complete, most perfect. That is why a wise philosopher has said,

"There is no greater or more perfect system of creation than that which already exists." ('Abdu'l-Bahá, *The Promulgation of Universal Peace,* pp. 109–10.)

Some of the celestial stars have a clear and apparent material effect upon the terrestrial globe and the earthly beings, which needs no explanation. Consider the sun, which through the aid and the providence of God develops the earth and all earthly beings. Without the light and heat of the sun, all the earthly creatures would be entirely nonexistent.

With regard to the spiritual influence of stars, though this influence of stars in the human world may appear strange, still, if you reflect deeply upon this subject, you will not be so much surprised at it. My meaning is not, however, that the decrees which the astrologers of former times inferred from the movements of the stars corresponded to occurrences; for the decrees of those former astrologers were forms of imagination which were originated by Egyptian, Assyrian and Chaldean priests; nay, rather, they were due to the fancies of Hindus, to the myths of the Greeks, Romans and other star worshipers. But I mean that this limitless universe is like the human body, all the members of which are connected and linked with one another with the greatest strength. How much the organs, the members and the parts of the body of man are intermingled and connected for mutual aid and help, and how much they influence one another! In the same way, the parts of this infinite universe have their members and elements connected with one another, and influence one another spiritually and materially.

For example, the eye sees, and all the body is affected; the ear hears, and all the members of the body are moved. Of this there is no doubt; and the universe is like a living person. Moreover, the connection which exists between the members of beings must necessarily have an effect and impression, whether it be material or spiritual.

For those who deny spiritual influence upon material things we mention this brief example: wonderful sounds and tones, melodies and charming voices, are accidents which affect the air—for sound is the term for vibrations of the air—and by these vibrations the nerves of the tympanum of the ear are affected, and hearing results. Now reflect that the vibration of the air, which is an accident of no importance, attracts and exhilarates the spirit of man and has great effect upon him: it makes him weep or laugh; perhaps it will influence him to such a degree that he will throw himself into danger. Therefore, see the connection which exists between the spirit of man and the atmospheric vibration, so that the movement of the air becomes the cause of transporting him from one state to another, and of entirely overpowering him; it will deprive him of patience and tranquility. Consider how strange this is, for nothing comes forth from the singer which enters into the listener; nevertheless, a great spiritual effect is produced. Therefore, surely so great a connection between beings must have spiritual effect and influence. ('Abdu'l-Bahá, *Some Answered Questions,* pp. 244–47.)

In the body of a man, . . . the spirit, when in ideal control of all the lesser parts of the organism, finds the utmost harmony throughout the whole body—each part is in perfect reciprocity with the other parts. The commands and impulses of the spirit are obeyed by the body and the body in turn in its actions and functions identifies and determines the expression the spiritual impulses shall take. This is divine unity—and this law, being universal and found in every created object in the universe, has full application to the universal Bahá'í organism made up of believers everywhere, which has been established by the Manifestation of God. (Shoghi Effendi, *Principles of Bahá'í Administration,* p. 2.)

We belong to an organic unit and when one part of the organism suffers all the rest of the body will feel its consequence. This is in fact the reason why Bahá'u'lláh calls our attention to the unity of mankind. (From a letter written on behalf of Shoghi Effendi, dated 14 April 1942, to a Bahá'í family, in *Lights of Guidance,* no. 446.)

PHYSICAL REALITY AS A METAPHORICAL GUIDE TO WELL-BEING AND SPIRITUAL TRUTH

Every created thing in the whole universe is but a door leading into His knowledge, a sign of His sovereignty, a revelation of His names, a symbol of His majesty, a token of His power, a means of admittance into His straight Path. (Bahá'u'lláh, *Gleanings from the Writings of Bahá'u'lláh,* no. 82.5.)

The spiritual world is like unto the phenomenal world. They are the exact counterpart of each other. Whatever objects appear in this world of existence are the outer pictures of the world of heaven. ('Abdu'l-Bahá, *The Promulgation of Universal Peace,* p. 12.)

[T]he outward is the expression of the inward; the earth is the mirror of the Kingdom; the material world corresponds to the spiritual world. ('Abdu'l-Bahá, *Some Answered Questions,* p. 283.)

The worlds of God are in perfect harmony and correspondence one with another. Each world in this limitless universe is, as it were, a mirror reflecting the history and nature of all the rest. The physical universe is, likewise, in perfect correspondence with the spiritual or divine realm. The world of matter is an outer expression or facsimile of the inner kingdom of spirit. The world of minds corresponds with the world of hearts. ('Abdu'l-Bahá, *The Promulgation of Universal Peace,* p. 377.)

Inasmuch as the fundamental principle of the teaching of Bahá'u'lláh is the oneness of the world of humanity, I will speak to you upon the intrinsic oneness of all phenomena. This is one of the abstruse subjects of divine philosophy.

Fundamentally all existing things pass through the same degrees and phases of development, and any given phenomenon embodies all others. An ancient statement of the Arabian philosophers declares that all things are involved in all things. It is evident that each material organism is an aggregate expression of single and simple elements, and a given cellular element or atom has its coursings or journeyings through various and myriad stages of life. . . . [E]ach phenomenon is the expression in degree of all other phenomena. The difference is one of successive transferences and the period of time involved in evolutionary process. . . .

The elements and lower organisms are synchronized in the great plan of life. Shall man, infinitely above them in degree, be antagonistic and a destroyer of that perfection? God forbid such a condition! ('Abdu'l-Bahá, *The Promulgation of Universal Peace,* pp. 493–94.)

Consider: Unity is necessary to existence. Love is the very cause of life; on the other hand, separation brings death. In the world of material creation, for instance, all things owe their actual life to unity. The elements which compose wood, mineral, or stone, are held together by the law of attraction. If this law should cease for one moment to operate these elements would not hold together, they would fall apart, and the object would in that particular form cease to exist. The law of attraction has brought together certain elements in the form of this beautiful flower, but when that attraction is withdrawn from this center the flower will decompose, and, as a flower, cease to exist.

So it is with the great body of humanity. The wonderful Law of Attraction, Harmony and Unity, holds together this marvelous Creation.

As with the whole, so with the parts; whether a flower or a human body, when the attracting principle is withdrawn from it, the flower or the man dies. It is therefore clear that attraction, harmony, unity and Love, are the cause of life, whereas repulsion, discord, hatred and separation bring death.

We have seen that whatever brings division into the world of existence causes death. Likewise in the world of the spirit does the same law operate. ('Abdu'l-Bahá, *Paris Talks*, no. 42.5–8.)

Consequently, that which is conducive to association and attraction and unity among the sons of men is the means of the life of the world of humanity, and whatever causeth division, repulsion and remoteness leadeth to the death of humankind. . . .

Consider the flowers of a garden: though differing in kind, color, form and shape, yet, inasmuch as they are refreshed by the waters of one spring, revived by the breath of one wind, invigorated by the rays of one sun, this diversity increaseth their charm, and addeth unto their beauty. . . . This diversity, this difference is like the naturally created dissimilarity and variety of the limbs and organs of the human body, for each one contributeth to the beauty, efficiency and perfection of the whole. ('Abdu'l-Bahá, *Selections from the Writings of 'Abdu'l-Bahá,* no. 225.19, 24.)

As preordained by the Fountainhead of Creation, the temple of the world hath been fashioned after the image and likeness of the human body. In fact each mirroreth forth the image of the other, wert thou but to observe with discerning eyes. By this is meant that even as the human body in this world which is outwardly composed of different limbs and organs, is in reality a closely integrated, coherent entity, similarly the structure of the physical world is like unto a single being whose limbs and members are inseparably linked together.

Were one to observe with an eye that discovereth the realities of all things, it would become clear that the greatest relationship that bindeth the world of being together lieth in the range of created things themselves, and that co-operation, mutual aid and reciprocity are essential characteristics in the unified body of the world of being, inasmuch as all created things are closely related together and each is influenced by the other or deriveth benefit therefrom, either directly or indirectly.

Consider for instance how one group of created things constituteth the vegetable kingdom, and another the animal kingdom. Each of these two maketh use of certain elements in the air on which its own life dependeth, while each increaseth the quantity of such elements as are essential for the life of the other. In other words, the growth and development of the vegetable world is impossible without the existence of the animal kingdom, and the maintenance of animal life is inconceivable without the co-operation of the vegetable kingdom. Of like kind are the relationships that exist among all created things. Hence it was stated that cooperation and reciprocity are essential properties which are inherent in the unified system of the world of existence, and without which the entire creation would be reduced to nothingness.

In surveying the vast range of creation thou shalt perceive that the higher a kingdom of created things is on the arc of ascent, the more conspicuous are the signs and evidences of the truth that co-operation and reciprocity at the level of a higher order are greater than those that exist at the level of a lower order. For example the evident signs of this fundamental reality are more discernible in the vegetable kingdom than in the mineral, and still more manifest in the animal world than in the vegetable.

And thus when contemplating the human world thou beholdest this wondrous phenomenon shining resplendent from all sides with the utmost perfection, inasmuch as in this station acts of cooperation, mutual assistance and reciprocity are not confined to the body and to things that pertain to the material world, but for all conditions, whether physical or spiritual, such as those related to minds, thoughts, opinions, manners, customs, attitudes, understandings, feelings or other human susceptibilities. In all these thou shouldst find these binding relationships securely established. The more this interrelationship is strengthened and expanded, the more will human society advance in progress and prosperity. Indeed without these vital ties it would be wholly impossible for the world of humanity to attain true felicity and success. ('Abdu'l-Bahá, in *Compilation of Compilations, Vol. I,* no. 1159.)

Know thou of a certainty that Love is the secret of God's holy Dispensation, the manifestation of the All-Merciful, the fountain of spiritual outpourings. Love is heaven's kindly light, the Holy Spirit's eternal breath that vivifieth the human soul. Love is the cause of God's revelation unto man, the vital bond inherent, in accordance with the divine creation, in the realities of things. Love is the one means that ensureth true felicity both in this world and the next. Love is the light that guideth in darkness, the living link that uniteth God with man, that assureth the progress of every illumined soul. Love is the most great law that ruleth this mighty and heavenly cycle, the unique power that bindeth together the divers elements of this material world, the supreme magnetic force that directeth the movements of the spheres in the celestial realms. Love revealeth with unfailing and limitless power the mysteries latent in the universe. Love is the spirit of life unto the adorned body of mankind, the establisher of true civilization in this mortal world, and the shedder of imperishable glory upon every high-aiming race and nation. ('Abdu'l-Bahá, *Selections from the Writings of 'Abdu'l-Bahá,* no. 12.1.)

We declare that love is the cause of the existence of all phenomena and that the absence of love is the cause of disintegration or nonexistence. Love is the conscious bestowal of God, the bond of affiliation in all phenomena. . . .

It is, therefore, evident that in the world of humanity the greatest king and sovereign is love. If love were extinguished, the power of attraction dispelled, the affinity of human hearts destroyed, the phenomena of human life would disappear. ('Abdu'l-Bahá, *The Promulgation of Universal Peace,* p. 356.)

If we look reflectively upon the material world, we realize that all outer phenomena are dependent upon the sun. Without the sun the phenomenal world would be in a state of utter darkness and devoid of life. All earthly creation—whether mineral, vegetable, animal or human—is dependent upon the heat, light and splendor of the great central solar body for training and development. Were it not for the solar heat and sunlight, no minerals would have been formed, no vegetable, animal and human organisms would or could have become existent. It is clearly evident, therefore, that the sun is the source of life to all earthly and outer phenomena.

In the inner world, the world of the Kingdom, the Sun of Reality is the Trainer and Educator of minds, souls and spirits. Were it not for the effulgent rays of the Sun of Reality, they would be deprived of growth and development; nay, rather, they would be nonexistent. For just as the physical sun is the trainer of all outer and phenomenal forms of being through the radiation of its light and heat, so the radiation of the light and heat of the Sun of Reality gives growth, education and evolution to minds, souls and spirits toward the station of perfection. ('Abdu'l-Bahá, *The Promulgation of Universal Peace,* pp. 377–78.)

Ascent and descent, stillness and motion, have come into being through the will of the Lord of all that hath been and shall be. The cause of ascent is lightness, and the cause of lightness is heat. Thus hath it been decreed by God. The cause of stillness is weight and density, which in turn are caused by coldness. Thus hath it been decreed by God.

And since He hath ordained heat to be the source of motion and ascent and the cause of attainment to the desired goal, He hath therefore kindled with the mystic hand that Fire that dieth not and sent it forth into the world, that this divine Fire might, by the heat of the love of God, guide and attract all mankind to the abode of the incomparable Friend. (Bahá'u'lláh, *The Pen of Glory,* no. 6.1–2.)

Creation is the expression of motion. Motion is life. A moving object is a living object, whereas that which is motionless and inert is as dead. All created forms are progressive in their planes, or kingdoms of existence, under the stimulus of the power or spirit of life. The universal energy is dynamic. Nothing is stationary in the material world of outer phenomena or in the inner world of intellect and consciousness.

Religion is the outer expression of the divine reality. Therefore, it must be living, vitalized, moving and progressive. If it be without motion and nonprogressive, it is without the divine life; it is dead. The divine institutes are continuously active and evolutionary; therefore, the revelation of them must be progressive and continuous. ('Abdu'l-Bahá, *The Promulgation of Universal Peace,* p. 191.)

When we look upon the phenomenal world, we perceive that it is divided into four seasons; one is the season of spring, another the season of summer, another autumn and then these three seasons are followed by winter. When the season of spring appears in the arena of existence, the whole world is rejuvenated and finds new life. . . .

The appearances of the Manifestations of God are the divine springtime. ('Abdu'l-Bahá, *The Promulgation of Universal Peace,* pp. 12–13.)

The physical sun has its rising and its setting. The earthly world has its day and its night. After each sunset there is a sunrise and the coming of a new dawn. The Sun of Reality, likewise, has its rising and setting. There is a day and a night in the world of spirituality.

After each departure there is a return and the dawning light of a new day. ('Abdu'l-Bahá, *The Promulgation of Universal Peace,* p. 379.)

Truth may be likened to the sun! The sun is the luminous body that disperses all shadows; in the same way does truth scatter the shadows of our imagination. As the sun gives life to the body of humanity so does truth give life to their souls. Truth is a sun that rises from different points on the horizon.

Sometimes the sun rises from the center of the horizon, then in summer it rises farther north, in winter farther south—but it is always the self-same sun, however different are the points of its rising.

In like manner truth is one, although its manifestations may be very different. Some men have eyes and see. These worship the sun, no matter from which point on the horizon it may dawn; and when the sun has left the winter sky to appear in the summer one, they know how to find it again. . . .

We must adore the sun itself and not merely the place of its appearance. In the same way men of enlightened heart worship truth on whatever horizon it appears. ('Abdu'l-Bahá, *Paris Talks,* no. 40.2–5.)

Know of a certainty that in every Dispensation the light of Divine Revelation hath been vouchsafed unto men in direct proportion to their spiritual capacity. Consider the sun. How feeble its rays the moment it appeareth above the horizon. How gradually its

warmth and potency increase as it approacheth its ze-
nith, enabling meanwhile all created things to adapt
themselves to the growing intensity of its light. How
steadily it declineth until it reacheth its setting point.
Were it, all of a sudden, to manifest the energies latent
within it, it would, no doubt, cause injury to all created things. . . . In like manner, if the Sun of Truth were
suddenly to reveal, at the earliest stages of its manifestation, the full measure of the potencies which the
providence of the Almighty hath bestowed upon it,
the earth of human understanding would waste away
and be consumed; for men's hearts would neither sus-
tain the intensity of its revelation, nor be able to mirror
forth the radiance of its light. Dismayed and overpow-
ered, they would cease to exist. (Bahá'u'lláh, *Gleanings
from the Writings of Bahá'u'lláh*, no. 38.1.)

All created things have their degree, or stage, of maturity. . . . The period of maturity in the life of a tree is
the time of its fruit bearing. The maturity of a plant
is the time of its blossoming and flower. The animal
attains a stage of full growth and completeness, and in
the human kingdom man reaches his maturity when
the lights of intelligence have their greatest power and
development.

From the beginning to the end of his life man passes through certain periods, or stages, each of which
is marked by certain conditions peculiar to itself. . . .

Similarly, there are periods and stages in the life of
the aggregate world of humanity, which at one time

was passing through its degree of childhood, at another its time of youth but now has entered its long presaged period of maturity, the evidences of which are everywhere visible and apparent. Therefore, the requirements and conditions of former periods have changed and merged into exigencies which distinctly characterize the present age of the world of mankind. That which was applicable to human needs during the early history of the race could neither meet nor satisfy the demands of this day and period of newness and consummation. Humanity has emerged from its former degrees of limitation and preliminary training. Man must now become imbued with new virtues and powers, new moralities, new capacities. ('Abdu'l-Bahá, *The Promulgation of Universal Peace,* pp. 617–18.)

The beginning of the existence of man on the terrestrial globe resembles his formation in the womb of the mother. The embryo in the womb of the mother gradually grows and develops until birth, after which it continues to grow and develop until it reaches the age of discretion and maturity. Though in infancy the signs of the mind and spirit appear in man, they do not reach the degree of perfection; they are imperfect. Only when man attains maturity do the mind and the spirit appear and become evident in utmost perfection.

So also the formation of man in the matrix of the world was in the beginning like the embryo; then gradually he made progress in perfectness, and grew and developed until he reached the state of maturity, when the mind and spirit became visible in the greatest power. In the beginning of his formation the mind and spirit also existed, but they were hidden; later they were manifested. . . .

All beings, whether large or small, were created perfect and complete from the first, but their perfections appear in them by degrees. . . .

For the supreme organization of God, and the universal natural system, surround all beings, and all are subject to this rule. ('Abdu'l-Bahá, *Some Answered Questions,* p. 198.)

Nonexistence, . . . is an expression applied to change of form, but this transformation can never be rightly considered annihilation, for the elements of composition are ever present and existent as we have seen in the journey of the atom through successive kingdoms, unimpaired; hence, there is no death; life is everlasting. So to speak, when the atom entered into the composition of the tree, it died to the mineral kingdom, and when consumed by the animal, it died to the vegetable kingdom, and so on until its transference or transmutation into the kingdom of man; but throughout its traversing it was subject to transformation and not annihilation. Death, therefore, is applicable to a change or transference from one degree or condition to another. ('Abdu'l-Bahá, *The Promulgation of Universal Peace,* p. 121.)

The nature of the soul after death can never be described, nor is it meet and permissible to reveal its whole character to the eyes of men. The Prophets and Messengers of God have been sent down for the sole purpose of guiding mankind to the straight Path of Truth. The purpose underlying Their revelation hath been to educate all men, that they may, at the hour of death, ascend, in the utmost purity and sanctity and with absolute detachment, to the throne of the Most High. The light which these souls radiate is responsible for the progress of the world and the advancement of its peoples. They are like unto leaven which leaveneth the world of being, and constitute the animating force through which the arts and wonders of the world are made manifest. Through them the clouds rain their bounty upon men, and the earth bringeth forth its fruits. All things must needs have a cause, a motive power, an animating principle. These souls and symbols of detachment have provided, and will continue to provide, the supreme moving impulse in the world of being. The world beyond is as different from this world as this world is different from that of the child while still in the womb of its mother. When the soul attaineth the Presence of God, it will assume the form that best befitteth its immortality and is worthy of its celestial habitation. (Bahá'u'lláh, *Gleanings from the Writings of Bahá'u'lláh*, no. 81.1.)

Now regarding the question whether the faculties of the mind and the human soul are one and the same. These faculties are but the inherent properties of the soul, such as the power of imagination, of thought, of understanding; powers that are the essential requisites of the reality of man, even as the solar ray is the inherent property of the sun. The temple of man is like unto a mirror, his soul is as the sun, and his mental faculties even as the rays that emanate from that source of light. The ray may cease to fall upon the mirror, but it can in no wise be dissociated from the sun. ('Abdu'l-Bahá, in *August Forel and the Bahá'í Faith,* pp. 24–25.)

The spirit of man must acquire its bounties from the Kingdom of God in order that it may become the mirror and manifestation of lights and the dawning point of divine traces, because the human reality is like the soil. If no bounty of rain descends from heaven upon the soil, if no heat of the sun penetrates, it will remain black, forbidding, unproductive; but when the moistening shower and the effulgent glow of the sun's rays fall upon it, beautiful and redolent flowers grow from its bosom. Similarly, the human spirit or reality of man, unless it becomes the recipient of the lights of the Kingdom, develops divine susceptibilities and consciously reflects the effulgence of God, will not be the manifestation of ideal bounties, for only the reality of man can become the mirror wherein the lights of God are revealed. ('Abdu'l-Bahá, *The Promulgation of Universal Peace,* p. 469.)

Be self-sacrificing in the path of God, and wing thy flight unto the heavens of the love of the Abhá

Beauty,* for any movement animated by love moveth from the periphery to the center, from space to the Daystar of the universe. Perchance thou deemest this to be difficult, but I tell thee that such cannot be the case, for when the motivating and guiding power is the divine force of magnetism it is possible, by its aid, to traverse time and space easily and swiftly. ('Abdu'l-Bahá, *Selections from the Writings of 'Abdu'l-Bahá,* no. 166.1.)

[A] proper appreciation of the laws of nature enables one to live in harmony with the forces of the planet. (From a letter written on behalf of the Universal House of Justice, dated 14 January 1985, to an individual believer, in *Lights of Guidance,* no. 1216.)

Just as there are laws governing our physical lives, requiring that we must supply our bodies with certain foods, maintain them within a certain range of temperatures, and so forth, if we wish to avoid physical disabilities, so also there are laws governing our spiritual lives. These laws are revealed to mankind in each age by the Manifestation of God, and obedience to them is of vital importance if each human being, and mankind in general, is to develop properly and harmoniously. Moreover, these various aspects are interdependent. If an individual violates the spiritual laws for his own development he will cause injury not only

---

* A title of Bahá'u'lláh, the Prophet and Founder of the Bahá'í Faith.

to himself but to the society in which he lives. Similarly, the condition of society has a direct effect on the individuals who must live within it. (The Universal House of Justice, *Messages from the Universal House of Justice, 1968–1973,* pp. 105–6.)

MIRACLES AND NATURAL LAWS

The meaning is not that the Manifestations are unable to perform miracles, for They have all power. But for Them inner sight, spiritual healing and eternal life are the valuable and important things. Consequently, whenever it is recorded in the Holy Books that such a one was blind and recovered his sight, the meaning is that he was inwardly blind, and that he obtained spiritual vision, or that he was ignorant and became wise, or that he was negligent and became heedful, or that he was worldly and became heavenly.

As this inner sight, hearing, life and healing are eternal, they are of importance. What, comparatively, is the importance, the value and the worth of this animal life with its powers? In a few days it will cease like fleeting thoughts. For example, if one relights an extinguished lamp, it will again become extinguished; but the light of the sun is always luminous. This is of importance. ('Abdu'l-Bahá, *Some Answered Questions,* p. 102.)

One thing, however, he wishes again to bring to your attention, namely that miracles are always possible, even though they do not constitute a regular channel whereby God reveals His power to mankind. To reject miracles on the ground that they imply a breach of the laws of nature is a very shallow, well-nigh a stupid argument, inasmuch as God Who is the Author of the universe can, in His Wisdom and Omnipotence, bring any change, no matter how temporary, in the operation of the laws which He Himself has created. (From a letter written on behalf of Shoghi Effendi, dated 27 February 1938, to an individual believer, in *Lights of Guidance,* no. 1638.)

Regarding the question you have asked in connection with a passage in Dr. Einstein's 'Cosmic Religion'; according to the Bahá'í conception there is and can be no incompatibility between the idea of causal law and that of an Omnipotent and Omniscient God, Who, if He deems it fit, may at times interfere with the normal sequence of events in the world, and thus retard or altogether stop the operation of certain laws, whether in the physical universe, or in any other worlds of nature and man. (From a letter written on behalf of Shoghi Effendi, dated 6 December 1939, to an individual believer, in *Lights of Guidance,* no. 1703.)

The belief in the possibilities of miracles, on the contrary, implies that God's power is beyond any limitation whatsoever. For it is only logical to believe that the Creator, Who is the sole Author of all the laws operating in the universe, is above them and can, therefore, if He deems it necessary, alter them at His Own

Will. We, as humans, cannot possibly attempt to read His Mind, and to fully grasp His Wisdom. Mystery is therefore an inseparable part of true religion, and as such, should be recognized by the believers. (From a letter of Shoghi Effendi, dated 1 October 1935, to an individual believer, in *Lights of Guidance,* no. 1641.)

Chapter Four:

CREATOR AND CREATION

OUT OF NOTHINGNESS

All praise to the unity of God, and all honor to Him, the sovereign Lord, the incomparable and all-glorious Ruler of the universe, Who, out of utter nothingness, hath created the reality of all things, Who, from naught, hath brought into being the most refined and subtle elements of His creation, and Who, rescuing His creatures from the abasement of remoteness and the perils of ultimate extinction, hath received them into His kingdom of incorruptible glory. Nothing short of His all-encompassing grace, His all-pervading mercy, could have possibly achieved it. How could it, otherwise, have been possible for sheer nothingness to have acquired by itself the worthiness and capacity to emerge from its state of non-existence into the realm of being? (Bahá'u'lláh, *Gleanings from the Writings of Bahá'u'lláh,* no. 27.1.)

The statement in the "Gleanings," . . . [extract no. 27.1] "who out of utter nothingness, . . ." etc., should be taken in a symbolic and not a literal sense. It is only to demonstrate the power and greatness of God. (From a letter written on behalf of Shoghi Effendi, *Letters from the Guardian to Australia and New Zealand, 1923–1957,* p. 41.)

THE UNITY OF GOD

Regard thou the one true God as One Who is apart from, and immeasurably exalted above, all created things. The whole universe reflecteth His glory, while He is Himself independent of, and transcendeth His creatures. This is the true meaning of Divine unity. He Who is the Eternal Truth is the one Power Who exerciseth undisputed sovereignty over the world of being, Whose image is reflected in the mirror of the entire creation. All existence is dependent upon Him, and from Him is derived the source of the sustenance of all things. This is what is meant by Divine unity; this is its fundamental principle. (Bahá'u'lláh, *Gleanings from the Writings of Bahá'u'lláh,* no. 84.1.)

THE IMAGE OF GOD IS
REFLECTED IN CREATION

Know thou that every created thing is a sign of the revelation of God. Each, according to its capacity, is, and will ever remain, a token of the Almighty. Inasmuch as He, the sovereign Lord of all, hath willed to reveal His sovereignty in the kingdom of names and attributes, each and every created thing hath, through the act of the Divine Will, been made a sign of His glory. So pervasive and general is this revelation that nothing whatsoever in the whole universe can be discovered that doth not reflect His splendor. Under such conditions every consideration of proximity and remoteness is obliterated. . . . Were the Hand of Divine power to divest of this high endowment all created things, the entire universe would become desolate and void. (Bahá'u'lláh, *Gleanings from the Writings of Bahá'u'lláh,* no. 93.1.)

CREATION IS PERFECT

When man looks at the beings with a penetrating regard, and attentively examines the condition of existences, and when he sees the state, the organization, and the perfection of the world, he will be convinced that in the possible world there is nothing more wonderful than that which already exists. For all existing beings, terrestrial and celestial, as well as this limitless space and all that is in it, have been created and organized, composed, arranged, and perfected as they ought to be; the universe has no imperfection; so that if all beings became pure intelligence and reflected for ever and ever, it is impossible that they could imagine anything better than that which exists. ('Abdu'l-Bahá, *Some Answered Questions,* p. 177.)

THE NONEXISTENCE OF EVIL IN GOD'S CREATION

In creation there is no evil; all is good. Certain qualities and natures innate in some men and apparently blameworthy are not so in reality. For example, from the beginning of his life you can see in a nursing child the signs of greed, of anger and of temper. Then, it may be said, good and evil are innate in the reality of man, and this is contrary to the pure goodness of nature and creation. The answer to this is that greed,

which is to ask for something more, is a praiseworthy quality provided that it is used suitably. So if a
man is greedy to acquire science and knowledge, or
to become compassionate, generous and just, it is
most praiseworthy. If he exercises his anger and wrath
against the bloodthirsty tyrants who are like ferocious
beasts, it is very praiseworthy; but if he does not use
these qualities in a right way, they are blameworthy.

Then it is evident that in creation and nature evil
does not exist at all; but when the natural qualities of
man are used in an unlawful way, they are blameworthy. ('Abdu'l-Bahá, *Some Answered Questions,* p. 214.)

Briefly, the intellectual realities, such as all the qualities and admirable perfections of man, are purely
good, and exist. Evil is simply their nonexistence. So
ignorance is the want of knowledge; error is the want
of guidance; forgetfulness is the want of memory; stu-
pidity is the want of good sense. All these things have
no real existence. . . .

Nevertheless a doubt occurs to the mind—that is,
scorpions and serpents are poisonous. Are they good
or evil, for they are existing beings? Yes, a scorpion is
evil in relation to man; a serpent is evil in relation to
man; but in relation to themselves they are not evil,
for their poison is their weapon, and by their sting
they defend themselves. But as the elements of their
poison do not agree with our elements—that is to
say, as there is antagonism between these different ele-

ments, therefore, this antagonism is evil; but in reality as regards themselves they are good.

The epitome of this discourse is that it is possible that one thing in relation to another may be evil, and at the same time within the limits of its proper being it may not be evil. Then it is proved that there is no evil in existence; all that God created He created good. ('Abdu'l-Bahá, *Some Answered Questions,* pp. 263–64.)

CREATION HAS NO BEGINNING OR END

A drop of the billowing ocean of His endless mercy hath adorned all creation with the ornament of existence, and a breath wafted from His peerless Paradise hath invested all beings with the robe of His sanctity and glory. A sprinkling from the unfathomed deep of His sovereign and all-pervasive Will hath, out of utter nothingness, called into being a creation which is infinite in its range and deathless in its duration. The wonders of His bounty can never cease, and the stream of His merciful grace can never be arrested. The process of His creation hath had no beginning, and can have no end. (Bahá'u'lláh, *Gleanings from the Writings of Bahá'u'lláh,* no. 26.2.)

Behold, how many are the mysteries that lie as yet unraveled within the tabernacle of the knowledge of God, and how numerous the gems of His wisdom that are still concealed in His inviolable treasuries! Shouldest thou ponder this in thine heart, thou wouldst realize that His handiwork knoweth neither beginning nor end. (Bahá'u'lláh, The Kitáb-i-Íqán, ¶178.)

Bahá'u'lláh says, "The universe hath neither beginning nor ending." He has set aside the elaborate theories and exhaustive opinions of scientists and material philosophers by the simple statement, "There is no beginning, no ending." The theologians and religionists advance plausible proofs that the creation of the universe dates back six thousand years; the scientists bring forth indisputable facts and say, "No! These evidences indicate ten, twenty, fifty thousand years ago," etc. There are endless discussions pro and con. Bahá'u'lláh sets aside these discussions by one word and statement. He says, "The divine sovereignty hath no beginning and no ending." By this announcement and its demonstration He has established a standard of agreement among those who reflect upon this question of divine sovereignty; He has brought reconciliation and peace in this war of opinion and discussion.

Briefly, there were many universal cycles preceding this one in which we are living. They were consummated, completed and their traces obliterated. The divine and creative purpose in them was the evolution of spiritual man, just as it is in this cycle. The circle of existence is the same circle; it returns. The tree of life has ever borne the same heavenly fruit. ('Abdu'l-Bahá, *The Promulgation of Universal Peace,* pp. 307–8.)

Notwithstanding this, we read in Genesis in the Old Testament that the lifetime of creation is but six thousand years. This has an inner meaning and significance; it is not to be taken literally. For instance, it is said in the Old Testament that certain things were created in the first day. The narrative shows that at that time the sun was not yet created. How could we conceive of a day if no sun existed in the heavens? For the day depends upon the light of the sun. Inasmuch as the sun had not been made, how could the first day be realized? Therefore, these statements have significances other than literal. ('Abdu'l-Bahá, *The Promulgation of Universal Peace,* p. 653.)

ALL CREATION IS PRECEDED BY A CAUSE

The one true God hath everlastingly existed, and will everlastingly continue to exist. His creation, likewise, hath had no beginning, and will have no end. All that is created, however, is preceded by a cause. This fact, in itself, establisheth, beyond the shadow of a doubt, the unity of the Creator. (Bahá'u'lláh, *Gleanings from the Writings of Bahá'u'lláh,* no. 82.10.)

Know that it is one of the most abstruse spiritual truths that the world of existence—that is to say, this endless universe—has no beginning.

We have already explained that the names and attributes of the Divinity themselves require the existence of beings. . . . If we could imagine a time when no beings existed, this imagination would be the denial of the Divinity of God. Moreover, absolute nonexistence cannot become existence. If the beings were absolutely nonexistent, existence would not have come into being. Therefore, as the Essence of Unity (that is, the existence of God) is everlasting and eternal—that is to say, it has neither beginning nor end—it is certain that this world of existence, this endless universe, has neither beginning nor end. Yes, it may be that one of the parts of the universe, one of the globes, for example, may come into existence, or may be disintegrated, but the other endless globes are still existing; the universe would not be disordered nor destroyed. On the contrary, existence is eternal and perpetual. . . .

It is necessary, therefore, that we should know what each of the important existences was in the beginning—for there is no doubt that in the beginning the origin was one: the origin of all numbers is one and not two. Then it is evident that in the beginning matter was one, and that one matter appeared in different aspects in each element. Thus various forms were produced, and these various aspects as they were produced became permanent, and each element was specialized. But this permanence was not definite, and did not attain realization and perfect existence until after a very long time. Then these elements became composed, and organized and combined in infinite forms; or rather from the composition and combination of these elements innumerable beings appeared.

This composition and arrangement, through the wisdom of God and His preexistent might, were produced from one natural organization, which was composed and combined with the greatest strength, conformable to wisdom, and according to a universal law. From this it is evident that it is the creation of God, and is not a fortuitous composition and arrangement. This is why from every natural composition a being can come into existence, but from an accidental composition no being can come into existence. For example, if a man of his own mind and intelligence collects some elements and combines them, a living being will not be brought into existence since the system is unnatural. This is the answer to the implied question that, since beings are made by the composition and the combination of elements, why is it not possible for us to gather elements and mingle them together, and so create a living being. This is a false supposition, for the origin of this composition is from God; it is God Who makes the combination, and as it is done according to the natural system, from each composition one being is produced, and an existence is realized. A composition made by man produces nothing because man cannot create. ('Abdu'l-Bahá, *Some Answered Questions,* pp. 180–82.)

Existence is of two kinds: one is the existence of God which is beyond the comprehension of man. He, the invisible, the lofty and the incomprehensible, is preceded by no cause but rather is the Originator of the cause of causes. He, the Ancient, hath had no beginning and is the all-independent. The second kind of existence is the human existence. It is a common existence, comprehensible to the human mind, is not ancient, is dependent and hath a cause to it. The mortal substance does not become eternal and vice versa; the human kind does not become a Creator and vice versa. The transformation of the innate substance is impossible. ('Abdu'l-Bahá, *Selections from the Writings of 'Abdu'l-Bahá,* no. 30.1.)

And now consider this infinite universe. Is it possible that it could have been created without a Creator? Or that the Creator and cause of this infinite congeries of worlds should be without intelligence? Is the idea tenable that the Creator has no comprehension of what is manifested in creation? Man, the creature, has volition and certain virtues. Is it possible that his Creator is deprived of these? A child could not accept this belief and statement. It is perfectly evident that man did not create himself and that he cannot do so. How could man of his own weakness create such a mighty being? Therefore, the Creator of man must be more perfect and powerful than man. If the creative cause of man be simply on the same level with man, then man himself should be able to create, whereas we know very well that we cannot create even our own likeness. Therefore, the Creator of man must be endowed with superlative intelligence and power in all points that creation involves and implies. ('Abdu'l-Bahá, *The Promulgation of Universal Peace,* p. 113.)

In fine, that Universal Reality with all its qualities and attributes that we recount is holy and exalted above all minds and understandings. As we, however, reflect with broad minds upon this infinite universe, we observe that motion without a motive force, and an effect without a cause are both impossible; that every being hath come to exist under numerous influences and continually undergoeth reaction. These influences, too, are formed under the action of still other influences. For instance, plants grow and flourish through the outpourings of vernal showers, whilst the cloud itself is formed under various other agencies and these agencies in their turn are reacted upon by still other agencies. For example, plants and animals grow and develop under the influence of what the philosophers of our day designate as hydrogen and oxygen and are reacted upon by the effects of these two elements; and these in turn are formed under still other influences. The same can be said of other beings whether they affect other things or be affected. Such process of causation goes on, and to maintain that this process goes on indefinitely is manifestly absurd. Thus such a chain of causation must of necessity lead eventually to Him who is the Ever-Living, the All-Powerful, who is Self-Dependent and the Ultimate Cause. This Universal Reality cannot be sensed, it cannot be seen. It must be so of necessity, for it is All-

Embracing, not circumscribed, and such attributes qualify the effect and not the cause. ('Abdu'l-Bahá, in *August Forel and the Bahá'í Faith,* p. 18.)

THE PROCESS OF CREATION

As regards thine assertions about the beginning of creation, this is a matter on which conceptions vary by reason of the divergences in men's thoughts and opinions. Wert thou to assert that it hath ever existed and shall continue to exist, it would be true; or wert thou to affirm the same concept as is mentioned in the sacred Scriptures, no doubt would there be about it, for it hath been revealed by God, the Lord of the worlds. Indeed He was a hidden treasure. This is a station that can never be described nor even alluded to. And in the station of "I did wish to make Myself known," God was, and His creation had ever existed beneath His shelter from the beginning that hath no beginning, apart from its being preceded by a Firstness which cannot be regarded as firstness and originated by a Cause inscrutable even unto all men of learning.

That which hath been in existence had existed before, but not in the form thou seest today. The world of existence came into being through the heat generated from the interaction between the active force and that which is its recipient. These two are the same, yet they are different. Thus doth the Great Announcement inform thee about this glorious structure. Such as communicate the generating influence and such as receive its impact are indeed created through the irresistible Word of God which is the Cause of the entire creation, while all else besides His Word are but the creatures and the effects thereof. Verily thy Lord is the Expounder, the All-Wise. (Bahá'u'lláh, *Tablets of Bahá'u'lláh,* p. 140.)

And as we consider the outpourings of Divine Grace we are assured of the existence of God. For instance, we observe that the existence of beings is conditioned upon the coming together of various elements and their non-existence upon the decomposition of their constituent elements. For decomposition causes the dissociation of the various elements. Thus, as we observe the coming together of elements giveth rise to the existence of beings, and knowing that beings are infinite, they being the effect, how can the Cause be finite?

Now, formation is of three kinds and of three kinds only: accidental, necessary and voluntary. The coming together of the various constituent elements of beings cannot be accidental, for unto every effect there must be a cause. It cannot be compulsory, for then the formation must be an inherent property of the constituent parts and the inherent property of a thing can in no wise be dissociated from it, such as light that is the revealer of things, heat that causeth the expansion of elements and the solar rays which are the essential property of the sun. Thus under such circumstances the decomposition of any formation is impossible, for the inherent properties of a thing cannot be separated from it. The third formation remaineth and that is the voluntary one, that is, an unseen force described as the Ancient Power, causeth these elements to come together, every formation giving rise to a distinct being. ('Abdu'l-Bahá, in *August Forel and the Bahá'í Faith,* pp. 16–17.)

WHY GOD CREATED HUMANITY

Having created the world and all that liveth and moveth therein, He, through the direct operation of His unconstrained and sovereign Will, chose to confer upon man the unique distinction and capacity to know Him and to love Him—a capacity that must needs be regarded as the generating impulse and the primary purpose underlying the whole of creation. . . . Upon the inmost reality of each and every created thing He hath shed the light of one of His names, and made it a recipient of the glory of one of His attributes. Upon the reality of man, however, He hath focused the radiance of all of His names and attributes, and made it a mirror of His own Self. Alone of all created things man hath been singled out for so great a favor, so enduring a bounty. (Bahá'u'lláh, *Gleanings from the Writings of Bahá'u'lláh,* no. 27.2.)

Thou didst wish to make Thyself known unto men; therefore, Thou didst, through a word of Thy mouth, bring creation into being and fashion the universe.

(Bahá'u'lláh, *Prayers and Meditations by Bahá'u'lláh*, p. 6.)

The supreme cause for creating the world and all that is therein is for man to know God. (Bahá'u'lláh, *Tablets of Bahá'u'lláh*, p. 267.)

It is clear and evident that when the veils that conceal the realities of the manifestations of the Names and Attributes of God, nay of all created things visible or invisible, have been rent asunder, nothing except the Sign of God will remain—a sign which He, Himself, hath placed within these realities. This sign will endure as long as is the wish of the Lord thy God, the Lord of the heavens and of the earth. If such be the blessings conferred on all created things, how superior must be the destiny of the true believer, whose existence and life are to be regarded as the originating purpose of all creation. (Bahá'u'lláh, *Gleanings from the Writings of Bahá'u'lláh*, no. 73.1.)

The cause of the creation of the phenomenal world is love. ('Abdu'l-Bahá, *The Promulgation of Universal Peace*, p. 414.)

For God is love, and all phenomena find source and emanation in that divine current of creation. The love of God haloes all created things. Were it not for the love of God, no animate being would exist. ('Abdu'l-Bahá, *The Promulgation of Universal Peace,* p. 448.)

THE ESSENCE OF GOD CANNOT BE COMPREHENDED

Every created being however revealeth His signs which are but emanations from Him and not His Own Self. All these signs are reflected and can be seen in the book of existence, and the scrolls that depict the shape and pattern of the universe are indeed a most great book. . . . Consider the rays of the sun whose light hath encompassed the world. The rays emanate from the sun and reveal its nature, but are not the sun itself. Whatsoever can be discerned on earth amply demonstrateth the power of God, His knowledge and the outpourings of His bounty, while He Himself is immeasurably exalted above all creatures. (Bahá'u'lláh, *Tablets of Bahá'u'lláh,* p. 60.)

The domain of His decree is too vast for the tongue of mortals to describe, or for the bird of the human mind to traverse; and the dispensations of His providence are too mysterious for the mind of man to comprehend. (Bahá'u'lláh, The Kitáb-i-Íqán, ¶178.)

So perfect and comprehensive is His creation that no mind nor heart, however keen or pure, can ever grasp the nature of the most insignificant of His creatures; much less fathom the mystery of Him Who is the Daystar of Truth, Who is the invisible and unknowable Essence. (Bahá'u'lláh, *Gleanings from the Writings of Bahá'u'lláh,* no. 26.3.)

The existence of the Divine Being hath been clearly established, on the basis of logical proofs, but the reality of the Godhead is beyond the grasp of the mind. When thou dost carefully consider this matter, thou wilt see that a lower plane can never comprehend a higher. The mineral kingdom, for example, which is lower, is precluded from comprehending the vegetable kingdom; for the mineral, any such understanding would be utterly impossible. In the same way, no matter how far the vegetable kingdom may develop, it will achieve no conception of the animal kingdom, and any such comprehension at its level would be unthinkable, for the animal occupieth a plane higher than that of the vegetable: this tree cannot conceive of hearing and sight. And the animal kingdom, no matter how far it may evolve, can never become aware of the reality of the intellect, which discovereth the inner essence of all things, and comprehendeth those realities which cannot be seen; for the human plane as compared with that of the animal is very high. . . .

The higher plane, however, understandeth the lower. The animal, for instance, comprehendeth the mineral and vegetable, the human understandeth the planes of the animal, vegetable and mineral. But the mineral cannot possibly understand the realms of man. And notwithstanding the fact that all these entities coexist in the phenomenal world, even so, no lower degree can ever comprehend a higher.

Then how could it be possible for a contingent reality, that is, man, to understand the nature of that pre-existent Essence, the Divine Being? The difference in station between man and the Divine Reality is thousands upon thousands of times greater than the difference between vegetable and animal. And that which a human being would conjure up in his mind is but the fanciful image of his human condition, it doth not encompass God's reality but rather is encompassed by it. ('Abdu'l-Bahá, *Selections from the Writings of 'Abdu'l-Bahá,* no. 21.2–4.)

Difference of condition is an obstacle to knowledge; the inferior degree cannot comprehend the superior degree. How then can the phenomenal reality comprehend the Preexistent Reality? Knowing God, therefore, means the comprehension and the knowledge of His attributes, and not of His Reality. ('Abdu'l-Bahá, *Some Answered Questions,* p. 221.)

What is meant by personal God is a God Who is conscious of His creation, Who has a Mind, a Will, a Purpose, and not, as many scientists and materialists believe, an unconscious and determined force operating in the universe. Such conception of the Divine Being, as the Supreme and ever present Reality in the world, is not anthropomorphic, for it transcends all human limitations and forms, and does by no means attempt to define the essence of Divinity which is obviously beyond any human comprehension. To say that God is a personal Reality does not mean that He has a physical form, or does in any way resemble a human being. To entertain such belief would be sheer blasphemy. (From a letter written on behalf of Shoghi Effendi, dated 21 April 1939, to an individual believer, in *Lights of Guidance,* no. 1574.)

KNOWING GOD THROUGH THE ATTRIBUTES AND TEACHINGS OF DIVINE MESSENGERS

And since there can be no tie of direct intercourse to bind the one true God with His creation, and no resemblance whatever can exist between the transient and the Eternal, the contingent and the Absolute, He hath ordained that in every age and dispensation a pure and stainless Soul be made manifest in the kingdoms of earth and heaven. Unto this subtle, this mysterious and ethereal Being He hath assigned a twofold nature; the physical, pertaining to the world of matter, and the spiritual, which is born of the substance of God Himself. He hath, moreover, conferred upon Him a double station. The first station, which is related to His innermost reality, representeth Him as One Whose voice is the voice of God Himself. . . . The second station is the human station, exemplified by the following verses: "I am but a man like you." . . . These Essences of Detachment, these resplendent Realities are the channels of God's all-pervasive grace. (Bahá'u'lláh, *Gleanings from the Writings of Bahá'u'lláh*, no. 27.4.)

These Tabernacles of holiness, these primal Mirrors which reflect the light of unfading glory, are but expressions of Him Who is the Invisible of the Invisibles. By the revelation of these gems of divine virtue all the names and attributes of God, such as knowledge and power, sovereignty and dominion, mercy and wisdom, glory, bounty and grace, are made manifest.

These attributes of God are not and have never been vouchsafed specially unto certain Prophets, and withheld from others. Nay, all the Prophets of God, His well-favored, His holy, and chosen Messengers, are, without exception, the bearers of His names, and the embodiments of His attributes. They only differ in the intensity of their revelation, and the comparative potency of their light. (Bahá'u'lláh, The Kitáb-i-Íqán, ¶109–10.)

Know thou assuredly that the essence of all the Prophets of God is one and the same. Their unity is absolute. God, the Creator, saith: There is no distinction whatsoever among the Bearers of My Message. (Bahá'u'lláh, *Gleanings from the Writings of Bahá'u'lláh,* no. 34.3.)

We find God only through the Intermediary of His Prophet. We see the Perfection of God in His Prophets. . . . God is never flesh, but mirrored in the attributes of His Prophets we see His Divine characteristics and perfections. (Shoghi Effendi, *High Endeavours: Messages to Alaska,* p. 70.)

The divinity attributed to so great a Being and the complete incarnation of the names and attributes of God in so exalted a Person should, under no circumstances, be misconceived or misinterpreted. The human temple that has been made the vehicle of so overpowering a Revelation must, if we be faithful to the tenets of our Faith, ever remain entirely distinguished from that "innermost Spirit of Spirits" and "eternal Essence of Essences"—that invisible yet rational God Who, however much we extol the divinity of His Manifestations on earth, can in no wise incarnate His infinite, His unknowable, His incorruptible and all-embracing Reality in the concrete and limited frame of a mortal being. Indeed, the God Who could so incarnate His own reality would, in the light of the teachings of Bahá'u'lláh, cease immediately to be God. So crude and fantastic a theory of Divine incarnation is as removed from, and incompatible with, the essentials of Bahá'í belief as are the no less inadmissible pantheistic and anthropomorphic conceptions of God—both of which the utterances of Bahá'u'lláh emphatically repudiate and the fallacy of which they expose. (Shoghi Effendi, *The World Order of Bahá'u'lláh*, p. 112.)

Any variations in the splendor which each of these Manifestations of the Light of God has shed upon the world should be ascribed not to any inherent superiority involved in the essential character of any one of them, but rather to the progressive capacity, the ever-increasing spiritual receptiveness, which mankind, in its progress towards maturity, has invariably manifested. (Shoghi Effendi, *The World Order of Bahá'u'lláh,* p. 166.)

Chapter Five:

OTHER
SCIENTIFIC SUBJECTS

ANIMALS

Briefly, it is not only their fellow human beings that the beloved of God must treat with mercy and compassion, rather must they show forth the utmost loving-kindness to every living creature. For in all physical respects, and where the animal spirit is concerned, the selfsame feelings are shared by animal and man. Man hath not grasped this truth, however, and he believeth that physical sensations are confined to human beings, wherefore is he unjust to the animals, and cruel.

And yet in truth, what difference is there when it cometh to physical sensations? The feelings are one and the same, whether ye inflict pain on man or on beast. There is no difference here whatever. And indeed ye do worse to harm an animal, for man hath a language, he can lodge a complaint, he can cry out and moan; if injured he can have recourse to the authorities and these will protect him from his aggressor. But the hapless beast is mute, able neither to express its hurt nor take its case to the authorities. If a man inflict a thousand ills upon a beast, it can neither ward him off with speech nor hale him into court. Therefore is it essential that ye show forth the utmost consideration to the animal, and that ye be even kinder to him than to your fellow man.

Train your children from their earliest days to be infinitely tender and loving to animals. If an animal be sick, let the children try to heal it, if it be hungry, let them feed it, if thirsty, let them quench its thirst, if weary, let them see that it rests. ('Abdu'l-Bahá, *Selections from the Writings of 'Abdu'l-Bahá,* no. 138.2–4.)

The honor and exaltation of every existing being depends upon causes and circumstances. The excellency, the adornment and the perfection of the earth is to be verdant and fertile through the bounty of the clouds of springtime. Plants grow; flowers and fragrant herbs spring up; fruit-bearing trees become full of blossoms and bring forth fresh and new fruit. Gardens become beautiful, and meadows adorned; mountains and plains are clad in a green robe, and gardens, fields, villages and cities are decorated. This is the prosperity of the mineral world.

The height of exaltation and the perfection of the vegetable world is that a tree should grow on the bank of a stream of fresh water, that a gentle breeze should blow on it, that the warmth of the sun should shine on it, that a gardener should attend to its cultivation, and that day by day it should develop and yield fruit. But its real prosperity is to progress into the animal and human world, and replace that which has been exhausted in the bodies of animals and men.

The exaltation of the animal world is to possess perfect members, organs and powers, and to have all its needs supplied. This is its chief glory, its honor and exaltation. So the supreme happiness of an animal is to have possession of a green and fertile meadow, perfectly pure flowing water, and a lovely, verdant forest. If these things are provided for it, no greater prosperity can be imagined. For example, if a bird builds its nest in a green and fruitful forest, in a beautiful high place, upon a strong tree, and at the top of a lofty branch, and if it finds all it needs of seeds and water, this is its perfect prosperity.

But real prosperity for the animal consists in passing from the animal world to the human world, like the microscopic beings that, through the water and air, enter into man and are assimilated, and replace that which has been consumed in his body. This is the great honor and prosperity for the animal world; no greater honor can be conceived for it. ('Abdu'l-Bahá, *Some Answered Questions,* p. 77.)

The distinctive virtue or plus of the animal is sense perception; it sees, hears, smells, tastes and feels but is incapable, in turn, of conscious ideation or reflection which characterizes and differentiates the human kingdom. The animal neither exercises nor apprehends this distinctive human power and gift. From the visible it cannot draw conclusions regarding the invisible, whereas the human mind from visible and known premises attains knowledge of the unknown and invisible. . . . The animal spirit cannot penetrate and discover the mysteries of things. It is a captive of the senses. No amount of teaching, for instance, would enable it to grasp the fact that the sun is stationary, and the earth moves around it. Likewise, the human spirit has its limitations. ('Abdu'l-Bahá, *The Promulgation of Universal Peace,* p. 79.)

Regarding the eating of animal flesh and abstinence therefrom, know thou of a certainty that, in the beginning of creation, God determined the food of every living being, and to eat contrary to that determination is not approved. For instance, beasts of prey, such as the wolf, lion and leopard, are endowed with ferocious, tearing instruments, such as hooked talons and claws. From this it is evident that the food of such beasts is meat. If they were to attempt to graze, their teeth would not cut the grass, neither could they chew the cud, for they do not have the molars. Likewise, God hath given to the four-footed grazing animals such teeth as reap the grass like sickle, and from this we understand that the food of these species of animal is vegetable. They cannot chase and hunt down other animals. The falcon hath a hooked beak and sharp talons; the hooked beak preventeth him from grazing, therefore his food also is meat. But now coming to man, we see he hath neither hooked teeth nor sharp nails or claws, nor teeth like iron sickles. From this it becometh evident and manifest that the food of man is cereals and fruit. Some of the teeth of man are like millstones to grind the grain, and some sharp to cut the fruit. Therefore he is not in need of meat, nor is he obliged to eat it. Even without eating meat he would with the utmost vigour and energy. For example, the community of the Brahmins in India do not eat meat; notwithstanding this they are not inferior to other nations in strength, power, vigour, outward senses or intellectual virtues. Truly, the killing of animals and the eating of their meat is somewhat contrary to pity and compassion, and if one can content oneself with cereals, fruit, oil and nuts, such as pistachios, almonds and so on, it would undoubtedly be better and more pleasing. (From a tablet of 'Abdu'l-Bahá, written to an individual believer, in *Lights of Guidance,* no. 1006.)

Atoms

Whatever is in the heavens and whatever is on the earth is a direct evidence of the revelation within it of the attributes and names of God, inasmuch as within every atom are enshrined the signs that bear eloquent testimony to the revelation of that Most Great Light. Methinks, but for the potency of that revelation, no being could ever exist. How resplendent the luminaries of knowledge that shine in an atom, and how vast the oceans of wisdom that surge within a drop! (Bahá'u'lláh, *Gleanings from the Writings of Bahá'u'lláh,* no. 27.4.)

[I]n each and every thing a door of knowledge hath been opened, and within every atom traces of the sun hath been made manifest. (Bahá'u'lláh, The Kitáb-i-Íqán, ¶28.)

How all-encompassing are the wonders of His boundless grace! Behold how they have pervaded the whole of creation. Such is their virtue that not a single atom in the entire universe can be found which doth not declare the evidences of His might, which doth not glorify His holy Name, or is not expressive of the effulgent light of His unity. (Bahá'u'lláh, *Gleanings from the Writings of Bahá'u'lláh,* no. 26.2.)

O SON OF BOUNTY! Out of the wastes of nothingness, with the clay of My command I made thee to appear, and have ordained for thy training every atom in existence and the essence of all created things. (Bahá'u'lláh, The Hidden Words, Persian, no. 29.)

Thou hast described thyself as a student in the school of spiritual progress. Fortunate art thou! If these schools of progress lead to the university of heaven, then branches of knowledge will be developed whereby humanity will look upon the tablet of existence as a scroll endlessly unfolding; and all created things will be seen upon that scroll as letters and words. Then will the different planes of meaning be learned, and then within every atom of the universe will be witnessed the signs of the oneness of God. ('Abdu'l-Bahá, *Selections from the Writings of 'Abdu'l-Bahá,* no. 29.2.)

If the atoms which compose the kingdom of the minerals were without affinity for each other, the earth would never have been formed, the universe could not have been created. Because they have affinity for each other, the power of life is able to manifest itself, and the organisms of the phenomenal world become possible. When this attraction or atomic affinity is destroyed, the power of life ceases to manifest; death and nonexistence result. ('Abdu'l-Bahá, *The Promulgation of Universal Peace,* p. 5.)

Life is the expression of composition; and death, the expression of decomposition. In the world or kingdom of the minerals certain materials or elemental substances exist. When through the law of creation they enter into composition, a being or organism comes into existence. For example, certain material atoms are brought together, and man is the result. When this composition is destroyed and disintegrated, decomposition takes place; this is mortality, or death. When certain elements are composed, an animal comes into being. When these elements are scattered or decomposed, this is called the death of the animal. Again, certain atoms are bound together by chemical affinity; a composition called a flower appears. When these atoms are dispersed and the composition they have formed is disintegrated, the flower has come to its end; it is dead. Therefore, it is evident that life is the expression of composition, and mortality, or death, is equivalent to decomposition. As the spirit of man is not composed of material elements, it is not subject to decomposition and, therefore, has no death. It is self-evident that the human spirit is simple, single and not composed in order that it may come to immortality, and it is a philosophical axiom that the individual or indivisible atom is indestructible. At most, it passes through a process of construction and reconstruction. ('Abdu'l-Bahá, *The Promulgation of Universal Peace,* pp. 425–26.)

Upon the faces of those present I behold the expression of thoughtfulness and wisdom; therefore, I shall discourse upon a subject involving one of the divine questions, a question of religious and metaphysical importance—namely, the progressive and perpetual motion of elemental atoms throughout the various degrees of phenomena and the kingdoms of existence. It will be demonstrated and become evident that the origin and outcome of phenomena are identical and that there is an essential oneness in all existing things. This is a subtle principle appertaining to divine philosophy and requiring close analysis and attention.

The elemental atoms which constitute all phenomenal existence and being in this illimitable universe are in perpetual motion, undergoing continuous degrees of progression. For instance, let us conceive of an atom in the mineral kingdom progressing upward to the kingdom of the vegetable by entering into the composition and fiber of a tree or plant. From thence it is assimilated and transferred into the kingdom of the animal and finally, by the law and process of composition, becomes a part of the body of man. That is to say, it has traversed the intermediate degrees and stations of phenomenal existence, entering into the composition of various organisms in its journey. This motion or transference is progressive and perpetual, for after disintegration of the human body into which it has entered, it returns to the mineral kingdom whence it came and will continue to traverse the kingdoms of phenomena as before. This is an illustration designed to show that the constituent elemental atoms of phenomena undergo progressive transference and motion throughout the material kingdoms.

In its ceaseless progression and journeyings the atom becomes imbued with the virtues and powers of each degree or kingdom it traverses. In the degree of the mineral it possessed mineral affinities; in the kingdom of the vegetable it manifested the augmentative virtue or power of growth; in the animal organism it reflected the intelligence of that degree; and in the kingdom of man it was qualified with human attributes or virtues.

Furthermore, the forms and organisms of phenomenal being and existence in each of the kingdoms of the universe are myriad and numberless. The vegetable plane or kingdom, for instance, has its infinite variety of types and material structures of plant life—each distinct and different within itself, no two exactly alike in composition and detail—for there are no repetitions in nature, and the augmentative virtue cannot be confined to any given image or shape. Each leaf has its own particular identity—so to speak, its own individuality as a leaf. Therefore, each atom of the innumerable elemental atoms, during its cease-less motion through the kingdoms of existence as a constituent of organic composition, not only becomes imbued with the powers and virtues of the kingdoms it traverses but also reflects the attributes and quali-ties of the forms and organisms of those kingdoms. As each of these forms has its individual and particular virtue, therefore, each elemental atom of the universe has the opportunity of expressing an infinite variety of those individual virtues. No atom is bereft or deprived of this opportunity or right of expression. Nor can it be said of any given atom that it is denied equal op-portunities with other atoms; nay, all are privileged to possess the virtues existent in these kingdoms and to reflect the attributes of their organisms. In the various transformations or passages from kingdom to king-dom the virtues expressed by the atoms in each degree are peculiar to that degree. For example, in the world of the mineral the atom does not express the vegetable form and organism, and when through the process of transmutation it assumes the virtues of the vegetable degree, it does not reflect the attributes of animal or-ganisms, and so on.

It is evident, then, that each elemental atom of the universe is possessed of a capacity to express all the virtues of the universe. ('Abdu'l-Bahá, *The Promulga-tion of Universal Peace,* pp. 396–98.)

Some define existence as the expression of reality or being and nonexistence as nonbeing, imagining that death is annihilation. This is a mistaken idea, for total annihilation is an impossibility. At most, composition is ever subject to decomposition or disintegration—that is to say, existence implies the grouping of material elements in a form or body, and nonexistence is simply the decomposing of these groupings. This is the law of creation in its endless forms and infinite variety of expression. Certain elements have formed the composite creature man. This composite association of the elements in the form of a human body is, therefore, subject to disintegration, which we call death, but after disintegration the elements themselves persist unchanged. Therefore, total annihilation is an impossibility, and existence can never become nonexistence. This would be equivalent to saying that light can become darkness, which is manifestly untrue and impossible. As existence can never become nonexistence, there is no death for man; nay, rather, man is everlasting and ever-living. The rational proof of this is that the atoms of the material elements are transferable from one form of existence to another, from one degree and kingdom to another, lower or higher. For example, an atom of the soil or dust of earth may traverse the kingdoms from mineral to man by successive incorporations into the bodies of the organisms of those kingdoms. At one time it enters into the formation of the mineral or rock; it is then absorbed by the vegetable kingdom and becomes a constituent of the body and fiber of a tree; again it is appropriated by the animal, and at a still later period is found in the body of man. Throughout these degrees of its traversing the kingdoms from one form of phenomenal being to another, it retains its atomic existence and is never annihilated nor relegated to nonexistence.

Nonexistence, therefore, is an expression applied to change of form, but this transformation can never be rightly considered annihilation, for the elements of composition are ever present and existent as we have seen in the journey of the atom through successive kingdoms, unimpaired; hence, there is no death; life is everlasting. ('Abdu'l-Bahá, *The Promulgation of Universal Peace,* pp. 120–21.)

Strange and astonishing things exist in the earth but they are hidden from the minds and the understanding of men. These things are capable of changing the whole atmosphere of the earth and their contamination would prove lethal. Great God! We have observed an amazing thing. Lightning or a force similar to it is controlled by an operator and moveth at his command. Immeasurably exalted is the Lord of Power Who hath laid bare that which He purposed through the potency of His weighty and invincible command. (Bahá'u'lláh, *Tablets of Bahá'u'lláh,* p. 69.)

The Words of Bahá'u'lláh regarding "a strange and wonderful instrument . . ." can, in the light of what Master said in San Francisco, so taken as a reference to the great destructive power atomic energy can be made to release. (From a letter written on behalf of Shoghi Effendi, dated 16 March 1946, to an individual believer, in *Lights of Guidance,* no. 1585.)

CELESTIAL SPHERES AND OTHER WORLDS

Thou hast, moreover, asked Me concerning the nature of the celestial spheres. To comprehend their nature, it would be necessary to inquire into the meaning of the allusions that have been made in the Books of old to the celestial spheres and the heavens, and to discover the character of their relationship to this physical world, and the influence which they exert upon it. Every heart is filled with wonder at so bewildering a theme, and every mind is perplexed by its mystery. God, alone, can fathom its import. The learned men, that have fixed at several thousand years the life of this earth, have failed, throughout the long period of their observation, to consider either the number or the age of the other planets. Consider, moreover, the manifold divergencies that have resulted from the theories propounded by these men. Know thou that every fixed star hath its own planets, and every planet its own creatures, whose number no man can compute. (Bahá'u'lláh, *Gleanings from the Writings of Bahá'u'lláh,* no. 82.11.)

Regarding the passage on p. 163 of the "Gleanings" [no. 82.11]; the creatures which Bahá'u'lláh states to be found in every planet cannot be considered to be necessarily similar or different from human beings on this earth. Bahá'u'lláh does not specifically state whether such creatures are like or unlike us. He simply refers to the fact that there are creatures in every planet. It remains for science to discover one day the exact nature of these creatures. (From a letter written on behalf of Shoghi Effendi to an individual believer, dated 9 February 1937, in *Lights of Guidance,* no. 1581.)

Verily I say, the creation of God embraceth worlds besides this world, and creatures apart from these creatures. In each of these worlds He hath ordained things which none can search except Himself, the All-Searching, the All-Wise. Do thou meditate on that which We have revealed unto thee, that thou mayest discover the purpose of God, thy Lord, and the Lord of all worlds. (Bahá'u'lláh, *Gleanings from the Writings of Bahá'u'lláh,* no. 76.1.)

Through His potency the Trees of Divine Revelation have yielded their fruits, every one of which hath been sent down in the form of a Prophet, bearing a Message to God's creatures in each of the worlds whose number God, alone, in His all-encompassing Knowledge, can reckon. (Bahá'u'lláh, *Gleanings from the Writings of Bahá'u'lláh,* no. 51.1.)

. . . 'Abdu'l-Bahá stated there are other worlds than ours which are inhabited by beings capable of knowing God. (Shoghi Effendi, *The Light of Divine Guidance, v. II,* p. 80.)

The earth has its inhabitants, the water and the air contain many living beings and all the elements have their nature spirits, then how is it possible to conceive that these stupendous stellar bodies are not inhabited? Verily, they are peopled, but let it be known that the dwellers accord with the elements of their respective spheres. These living beings do not have states of consciousness like unto those who live on the surface of this globe: the power of adaptation and environment moulds their bodies and states of consciousness, just as our bodies and minds are suited to our planet.

For example, we have birds that live in the air, those that live on the earth and those that live in the sea. The sea birds are adapted to their elements, likewise the birds which soar in the air, and those which hover about the earth's surface. Many animals living on the land have their counterparts in the sea. The domestic horse has his counterpart in the sea-horse which is half horse and half fish.

The components of the sun differ from those of this earth, for there are certain light and life-giving elements radiating from the sun. Exactly the same elements may exist in two bodies, but in varying quantities. For instance, there is fire and air in water, but the allotted measure is small in proportion.

They have discovered that there is a great quantity of radium in the sun; the same element is found on the earth, but in a much smaller degree. Beings who inhabit those distant luminous bodies are attuned to the elements that have gone into the composition of their respective spheres. ('Abdu'l-Bahá, quoted by the Research Department of the Universal House of Justice, 8 June 1992, "Gaia Concept, Nature," p. 11.)

As to your question whether the power of Bahá'u'lláh extends over our solar system and to higher worlds: while the Revelation of Bahá'u'lláh, it should be noted, is primarily for this planet, yet the spirit animating it is all-embracing, and the scope therefore cannot be restricted or defined. (From a letter written on behalf of the Guardian to an individual believer, dated 14 July 1938, in *Lights of Guidance,* no. 1594.)

Regarding your questions: There is no record in history, or in the teachings, of a Prophet similar in Station to Bahá'u'lláh, having lived 500,000 years ago. There will, however, be one similar to Him in greatness after the lapse of 500,000 years, but we cannot say definitely that His Revelation will be inter-planetary in scope. We can only say that such a thing may be possible. What Bahá'u'lláh means by His appearance in "other worlds" He has not defined, as we could not visualize them in our present state, hence He was indefinite, and we cannot say whether He meant other planets or not. (From a letter written on behalf of Shoghi Effendi to an individual believer, dated 24 December 1941, in *Lights of Guidance,* no. 1955.)

One thing he can assure you however is that there is nothing in the Bahá'í Faith about flying saucers. (From a letter written on behalf of Shoghi Effendi to an individual believer, in *Messages to the Antipodes*, p. 426.)

As you rightly state, Bahá'u'lláh affirms that every fixed star has its planets, and every planet its own creatures. The House of Justice states however, that it has not discovered anything in the Bahá'í Writings which would indicate the degree of progress such creatures may have attained. Obviously, as creatures of earth have managed to construct space probes and send them into outer space, it can be believed that creatures on other planets may have succeeded in doing likewise.

Regarding the attitude Bahá'ís should take toward unidentified flying objects, the House of Justice points out that they fall in the category of subjects open to scientific investigation, and as such, may be of interest to some, but not necessarily to everyone. (From a letter written on behalf of the Universal House of Justice to an individual believer, dated 11 January 1982.)

DIVERSITY

Nature in its essence is the embodiment of My Name, the Maker, the Creator. Its manifestations are diversified by varying causes, and in this diversity there are signs for men of discernment. (Bahá'u'lláh, *Tablets of Bahá'u'lláh*, p. 142.)

Consider the flowers of a garden: though differing in kind, color, form and shape, yet, inasmuch as they are refreshed by the waters of one spring, revived by the breath of one wind, invigorated by the rays of one sun, this diversity increaseth their charm, and addeth unto their beauty. Thus when that unifying force, the penetrating influence of the Word of God, taketh effect, the difference of customs, manners, habits, ideas, opinions and dispositions embellisheth the world of humanity. This diversity, this difference is like the naturally created dissimilarity and variety of the limbs and organs of the human body, for each one contributeth to the beauty, efficiency and perfection of the whole. When these different limbs and organs come under the influence of man's sovereign soul, and the soul's power pervadeth the limbs and members, veins and arteries of the body, then difference reinforceth harmony, diversity strengtheneth love, and multiplicity is the greatest factor for coordination.

How unpleasing to the eye if all the flowers and plants, the leaves and blossoms, the fruits, the branches and the trees of that garden were all of the same shape and color! Diversity of hues, form and shape, enricheth and adorneth the garden, and heighteneth the effect thereof. ('Abdu'l-Bahá, *Selections from the Writings of 'Abdu'l-Bahá,* no. 225.14–15.)

Consider the world of created beings, how varied and diverse they are in species, yet with one sole origin. All the differences that appear are those of outward form and color. This diversity of type is apparent throughout the whole of nature.

Behold a beautiful garden full of flowers, shrubs, and trees. Each flower has a different charm, a peculiar beauty, its own delicious perfume and beautiful color. The trees too, how varied are they in size, in growth, in foliage—and what different fruits they bear! Yet all these flowers, shrubs and trees spring from the self-same earth, the same sun shines upon them and the same clouds give them rain.

So it is with humanity. It is made up of many races, and its peoples are of different color, white, black, yellow, brown and red—but they all come from the same God, and all are servants to Him. This diversity among the children of men has unhappily not the same effect as it has among the vegetable creation, where the spirit shown is more harmonious. ('Abdu'l-Bahá, *Paris Talks,* no. 15.3–5.)

Now ponder this: Animals, despite the fact that they lack reason and understanding, do not make colors the cause of conflict. Why should man, who has reason, create conflict? This is wholly unworthy of him. Especially white and black are the descendants of the same Adam; they belong to one household. In origin they were one; they were the same color. Adam was of one color. Eve had one color. All humanity is descended from them. Therefore, in origin they are one. These colors developed later due to climates and regions; they have no significance whatsoever. ('Abdu'l-Bahá, *The Promulgation of Universal Peace,* p. 45.)

It is clear that the reality of mankind is diverse, that opinions are various and sentiments different; and this difference of opinions, of thoughts, of intelligence, of sentiments among the human species arises from essential necessity; for the differences in the degrees of existence of creatures is one of the necessities of existence, which unfolds itself in infinite forms. ('Abdu'l-Bahá, *Some Answered Questions,* p. 301.)

'Abdu'l-Bahá has written that the more distant the blood-relationship between the couple the better, since such marriages provide the basis for the physical well-being of humanity and are conducive to fellowship among mankind. (The Universal House of Justice, Notes to The Kitáb-i-Aqdas, no. 133, p. 222.)

God's wisdom hath decreed that partners to a marriage should be of distant origins. That is, the further removed the relationship between husband wife is, the stronger, the more beautiful and the healthier will their offspring be. ('Abdu'l-Bahá, in *The Pupil of the Eye,* p. 66.)

The Bahá'í Faith seeks to maintain cultural diversity while promoting the unity of all peoples. Indeed, such diversity will enrich the tapestry of human life in a peaceful world society. (The Universal House of Justice, in *The Pupil of the Eye,* p. 73.)

EARTH AND ECOLOGY
Every man of discernment, while walking upon the earth, feeleth indeed abashed, inasmuch as he is fully

aware that the thing which is the source of his prosperity, his wealth, his might, his exaltation, his advancement and power is, as ordained by God, the very
earth which is trodden beneath the feet of all men.
There can be no doubt that whoever is cognizant of
this truth, is cleansed and sanctified from all pride,
arrogance, and vainglory. (Bahá'u'lláh, Epistle to the
Son of the Wolf, p. 44.)

What is it of which ye can rightly boast? Is it on your
food and your drink that ye pride yourselves, on the
riches ye lay up in your treasuries, on the diversity and
the cost of the ornaments with which ye deck yourselves? If true glory were to consist in the possession
of such perishable things, then the earth on which ye
walk must needs vaunt itself over you, because it sup-
plieth you, and bestoweth upon you, these very things,
by the decree of the Almighty. In its bowels are contained, according to what God hath ordained, all that
ye possess. From it, as a sign of His mercy, ye derive
your riches. Behold then your state, the thing in which
ye glory! Would that ye could perceive it. (Bahá'u'lláh,
Gleanings from the Writings of Bahá'u'lláh, no. 143.7.)

As to thy question whether the physical world is subject to any limitations, know thou that the comprehension of this matter dependeth upon the observer
himself. In one sense, it is limited; in another, it is
exalted beyond all limitations. (Bahá'u'lláh, *Gleanings
from the Writings of Bahá'u'lláh,* no. 82.10.)

[T]his terrestrial globe, having once found existence, grew and developed in the matrix of the universe, and came forth in different forms and conditions, until gradually it attained this present perfection, and became adorned with innumerable beings, and appeared as a finished organization. ('Abdu'l-Bahá, *Some Answered Questions,* p. 182.)

Each one of the luminous bodies in this limitless firmament has a cycle of revolution which is of a different duration, and every one revolves in its own orbit, and again begins a new cycle. So the earth, every three hundred and sixty-five days, five hours, forty-eight minutes and a fraction, completes a revolution; and then it begins a new cycle—that is to say, the first cycle is again renewed. In the same way, for the whole universe, whether for the heavens or for men, there are cycles of great events, of important facts and occurrences. When a cycle is ended, a new cycle begins; and the old one, on account of the great events which take place, is completely forgotten, and not a trace or record of it will remain. As you see, we have no records of twenty thousand years ago, although we have before proved by argument that life on this earth is very ancient. It is not one hundred thousand, or two hundred thousand, or one million or two million years old; it is very ancient, and the ancient records and traces are entirely obliterated. ('Abdu'l-Bahá, *Some Answered Questions,* p. 160.)

This world is full of seeming contradictions; in each of these kingdoms (mineral, vegetable and animal) life exists in its degree; though when compared to the life in a man, the earth appears to be dead, yet she, too, lives and has a life of her own. ('Abdu'l-Bahá, *Paris Talks*, no. 20.14.)

We need a change of heart, a reframing of all our conceptions and a new orientation of our activities. The inward life of man as well as his outward environment have to be reshaped if human salvation is to be secured. (Shoghi Effendi, in *The Compilation of Compilations*, vol. 1, p. 85.)

We cannot segregate the human heart from the environment outside us and say that once one of these is reformed everything will be improved. Man is organic with the world. His inner life moulds the environment and is itself also deeply affected by it. The one acts upon the other and every abiding change in the life of man is the result of these mutual reactions.

No movement in the world directs its attention upon both these aspects of human life and has full measures for their improvement, save the teachings of Bahá'u'lláh. And this is its distinctive feature. (Shoghi Effendi, in *The Compilation of Compilations*, vol. I, p. 84.)

Creation reflects the names and attributes of God, and mankind has a profound responsibility to protect the natural environment and preserve its ecological balance. (The Universal House of Justice, in *The True Foundation of All Economics,* p. 117.)

Until such time as the nations of the world understand and follow the admonitions of Bahá'u'lláh to wholeheartedly work together in looking after the best interests of all humankind, and unite in the search for ways and means to meet the many environmental problems besetting our planet, the House of Justice feels that little progress will be made towards their solution. (The Universal House of Justice, in *The Compilation of Compilations,* vol. I, p. 85.)

EVOLUTION

No created thing shall ever attain its paradise unless it appeareth in its highest prescribed degree of perfection. For instance, this crystal representeth the paradise of the stone whereof its substance is composed. Likewise there are various stages in the paradise for the crystal itself. . . . So long as it was stone it was worthless, but if it attaineth the excellence of ruby—a potentiality which is latent in it—how much a carat will it be worth? Consider likewise every created thing. (The Báb, *Selections from the Writings of the Báb,* no. 3:15:1.)

In the physical creation, evolution is from one degree of perfection to another. The mineral passes with its mineral perfections to the vegetable; the vegetable, with its perfections, passes to the animal world, and so on to that of humanity. ('Abdu'l-Bahá, *Paris Talks,* no. 20.14.)

The beginning of the existence of man on the terrestrial globe resembles his formation in the womb of the mother. The embryo in the womb of the mother gradually grows and develops until birth, after which it continues to grow and develop until it reaches the age of discretion and maturity. Though in infancy the signs of the mind and spirit appear in man, they do not reach the degree of perfection; they are imperfect. Only when man attains maturity do the mind and the spirit appear and become evident in utmost perfection.

So also the formation of man in the matrix of the world was in the beginning like the embryo; then gradually he made progress in perfectness, and grew and developed until he reached the state of maturity, when the mind and spirit became visible in the greatest power. In the beginning of his formation the mind and spirit also existed, but they were hidden; later they were manifested. In the womb of the world mind and spirit also existed in the embryo, but they were concealed; afterward they appeared. So it is that in the seed the tree exists, but it is hidden and concealed; when it develops and grows, the complete tree appears. In the same way the growth and development of all beings is gradual; this is the universal divine organization and the natural system. The seed does not at once become a tree; the embryo does not at once become a man; the mineral does not suddenly become a stone. No, they grow and develop gradually and attain the limit of perfection.

All beings, whether large or small, were created perfect and complete from the first, but their perfections appear in them by degrees. The organization of God is one; the evolution of existence is one; the divine system is one. Whether they be small or great beings, all are subject to one law and system. Each seed has in it from the first all the vegetable perfections. For example, in the seed all the vegetable perfections exist from the beginning, but not visibly; afterward little by little they appear. So it is first the shoot which appears from the seed, then the branches, leaves, blossoms and fruits; but from the beginning of its existence all these things are in the seed, potentially, though not apparently.

In the same way, the embryo possesses from the first all perfections, such as the spirit, the mind, the sight, the smell, the taste—in one word, all the powers—but they are not visible and become so only by degrees.

Similarly, the terrestrial globe from the beginning was created with all its elements, substances, minerals, atoms and organisms; but these only appeared by degrees: first the mineral, then the plant, afterward the animal, and finally man. But from the first these kinds and species existed, but were undeveloped in the terrestrial globe, and then appeared only gradually. For the supreme organization of God, and the universal natural system, surround all beings, and all are subject to this rule. When you consider this universal system, you see that there is not one of the beings which at its coming into existence has reached the limit of perfection. No, they gradually grow and develop, and then attain the degree of perfection. ('Abdu'l-Bahá, *Some Answered Questions,* p. 198.)

. . . man, being the culmination of all that went before and thus superior to all previous evolutions, contains all the lower world within himself. Illumined by the spirit through the instrumentality of the soul, man's radiant intelligence makes him the crowning-point of Creation. ('Abdu'l-Bahá, *Paris Talks,* no. 121.5.)

In the world of existence man has traversed successive degrees until he has attained the human kingdom. In each degree of his progression he has developed capacity for advancement to the next station and condition. While in the kingdom of the mineral he was attaining the capacity for promotion into the degree of the vegetable. In the kingdom of the vegetable he underwent preparation for the world of the animal, and from thence he has come onward to the human degree, or kingdom. Throughout this journey of progression he has ever and always been potentially man. ('Abdu'l-Bahá, *The Promulgation of Universal Peace,* p. 315.)

Question. — What do you say with regard to the theories held by some European philosophers on the growth and development of beings?

Answer. — This subject was spoken of the other day, but we will speak of it again. Briefly, this question will be decided by determining whether species are original or not—that is to say, has the species of man been established from its origin, or was it afterward derived from the animals?

Certain European philosophers agree that the species grows and develops, and that even change and alteration are also possible. One of the proofs that they give for this theory is that through the attentive study and verification of the science of geology it has become clear that the existence of the vegetable preceded that of the animal, and that of the animal preceded that of man. They admit that both the vegetable and the animal species have changed, for in some of the strata of the earth they have discovered plants which existed in the past and are now extinct; they have progressed, grown in strength, their form and appearance have changed, and so the species have altered. In the same way, in the strata of the earth there are some species of animals which have changed and are transformed. One of these animals is the serpent. There are indications that the serpent once had feet, but through the lapse of time those members have disappeared. In the same way, in the vertebral column of man there is an indication which amounts to a proof that, like other animals, he once had a tail. At one time that member was useful, but when man developed, it was no longer of use; and, therefore, it gradually disappeared. As the serpent took refuge under the ground and became a creeping animal, it was no longer in need of feet, so they disappeared; but their traces survive. The principal argument is this: that the existence of traces of members proves that they once existed, and as now they are no longer of service, they have gradually disappeared. Therefore, while the perfect and necessary members have remained, those which are unnecessary have gradually disappeared by the modification of the species, but the traces of them continue.

The first answer to this argument is the fact that the animal having preceded man is not a proof of the evolution, change and alteration of the species, nor that man was raised from the animal world to the human world. For while the individual appearance of these different beings is certain, it is possible that man came into existence after the animal. So when we examine the vegetable kingdom, we see that the fruits of the different trees do not arrive at maturity at one time; on the contrary, some come first and others afterward. This priority does not prove that the later fruit of one tree was produced from the earlier fruit of another tree.

Second, these slight signs and traces of members have perhaps a great reason of which the mind is not yet cognizant. How many things exist of which we do not yet know the reason! So the science of physiology—that is to say, the knowledge of the composition of the members—records that the reason and cause of the difference in the colors of animals, and of the hair of men, of the redness of the lips, and of the variety of the colors of birds, is still unknown; it is secret and hidden. But it is known that the pupil of the eye is black so as to attract the rays of the sun, for if it were another color—that is, uniformly white—it would not attract the rays of the sun. Therefore, as the reason of the things we have mentioned is unknown, it is possible that the reason and the wisdom of these traces of members, whether they be in the animal or man, are equally unknown. Certainly there is a reason, even though it is not known.

Third, let us suppose that there was a time when some animals, or even man, possessed some members which have now disappeared; this is not a sufficient proof of the change and evolution of the species. For man, from the beginning of the embryonic period till he reaches the degree of maturity, goes through different forms and appearances. His aspect, his form, his appearance and color change; he passes from one form to another, and from one appearance to another. Nevertheless, from the beginning of the embryonic period he is of the species of man—that is to say, an embryo of a man and not of an animal; but this is not at first apparent, but later it becomes visible and evident. For example, let us suppose that man once resembled the animal, and that now he has progressed and changed. Supposing this to be true, it is still not a proof of the change of species. No, as before mentioned, it is merely like the change and alteration of the embryo of man until it reaches the degree of reason and perfection. We will state it more clearly. Let us suppose that there was a time when man walked on his hands and feet, or had a tail; this change and alteration is like that of the fetus in the womb of the mother. Although it changes in all ways, and grows and develops until it reaches the perfect form, from the beginning it is a special species. We also see in the vegetable kingdom that the original species of the genus do not change and alter, but the form, color and bulk will change and alter, or even progress.

To recapitulate: as man in the womb of the mother passes from form to form, from shape to shape, changes and develops, and is still the human species from the beginning of the embryonic period—in the same way man, from the beginning of his existence in the matrix of the world, is also a distinct species—that is, man—and has gradually evolved from one form to another. Therefore, this change of appearance, this evolution of members, this development and growth, even though we admit the reality of growth and progress, does not prevent the species from being original. Man from the beginning was in this perfect form and composition, and possessed capacity and aptitude for acquiring material and spiritual perfections, and was the manifestation of these words, "We will make man in Our image and likeness." ('Abdu'l-Bahá, *Some Answered Questions,* p. 191.)

The philosophers of the Orient in reply to those of the western world say: Let us suppose that the human anatomy was primordially different from its present form, that it was gradually transformed from one stage to another until it attained its present likeness, that at one time it was similar to a fish, later an invertebrate and finally human. This anatomical evolution or progression does not alter or affect the statement that the development of man was always human in type and biological in progression. For the human embryo when examined microscopically is at first a mere germ or worm. Gradually as it develops it shows certain divisions; rudiments of hands and feet appear—that is to say, an upper and a lower part are distinguishable. Afterward it undergoes certain distinct changes until it reaches its actual human form and is born into this world. But at all times, even when the embryo resembled a worm, it was human in potentiality and character, not animal. The forms assumed by the human embryo in its successive changes do not prove that it is animal in its essential character. Throughout this progression there has been a transference of type, a conservation of species or kind. Realizing this we may acknowledge the fact that at one time man was an inmate of the sea, at another period an invertebrate, then a vertebrate and finally a human being standing erect. Though we admit these changes, we cannot say man is an animal. In each one of these stages are signs and evidences of his human existence and destination. Proof of this lies in the fact that in the embryo man still resembles a worm. This embryo still progresses from one state to another, assuming different forms until that which was potential in it—namely, the human image—appears. Therefore, in the protoplasm, man is man. Conservation of species demands it.

The lost link of Darwinian theory is itself a proof that man is not an animal. How is it possible to have all the links present and that important link absent? Its absence is an indication that man has never been an animal. It will never be found. ('Abdu'l-Bahá, *The Promulgation of Universal Peace*, pp. 506–7.)

We cannot prove man was always man for this is a fundamental doctrine, but it is based on the assertion that nothing can exceed its own potentialities, that everything, a stone, a tree, an animal and a human being existed in plan, potentially, from the very "beginning" of creation. We don't believe man has always had the form of man, but rather that from the outset he was going to evolve into the human form and species and not be a haphazard branch of the ape family.

You see our whole approach to each matter is based on the belief that God sends us divinely inspired Educators; what they tell us is fundamentally true, what science tells us today is true; tomorrow may be entirely changed to better explain a new set of facts. (From a letter written on behalf of Shoghi Effendi, dated 7 June 1946, in *Arohanui: Letters to New Zealand*, p. 85.)

From the beginning to the end of his life man passes through certain periods, or stages, each of which is marked by certain conditions peculiar to itself. For instance, during the period of childhood his conditions and requirements are characteristic of that degree of intelligence and capacity. After a time he enters the period of youth, in which his former conditions and needs are superseded by new requirements applicable to the advance in his degree. His faculties of observation are broadened and deepened; his intelligent capacities are trained and awakened; the limitations and environment of childhood no longer restrict his energies and accomplishments. At last he passes out of the period of youth and enters the stage, or station, of maturity, which necessitates another transformation and corresponding advance in his sphere of life activity. New powers and perceptions clothe him, teaching and training commensurate with his progression occupy his mind, special bounties and bestowals descend in proportion to his increased capacities, and his former period of youth and its conditions will no longer satisfy his matured view and vision.

Similarly, there are periods and stages in the life of the aggregate world of humanity, which at one time was passing through its degree of childhood, at another its time of youth but now has entered its long presaged period of maturity, the evidences of which are everywhere visible and apparent. Therefore, the requirements and conditions of former periods have changed and merged into exigencies which distinctly characterize the present age of the world of mankind. That which was applicable to human needs during the early history of the race could neither meet nor satisfy the demands of this day and period of newness and consummation. Humanity has emerged from its former degrees of limitation and preliminary training. Man must now become imbued with new virtues and powers, new moralities, new capacities. New bounties, bestowals and perfections are awaiting and already descending upon him. The gifts and graces of the period of youth, although timely and sufficient during the adolescence of the world of mankind, are now incapable of meeting the requirements of its maturity. The playthings of childhood and infancy no longer satisfy or interest the adult mind. ('Abdu'l-Bahá, *The Promulgation of Universal Peace*, pp. 617–18.)

From every standpoint the world of humanity is undergoing a reformation. The laws of former governments and civilizations are in process of revision; scientific ideas and theories are developing and advancing to meet a new range of phenomena; invention and discovery are penetrating hitherto unknown fields, revealing new wonders and hidden secrets of the material universe; industries have vastly wider scope and production; everywhere the world of mankind is in the throes of evolutionary activity indicating the passing of the old conditions and advent of the new age of reformation. Old trees yield no fruitage; old ideas and methods are obsolete and worthless now. Old standards of ethics, moral codes and methods of living in the past will not suffice for the present age of advancement and progress. ('Abdu'l-Bahá, *The Promulgation of Universal Peace*, p. 618.)

When a divine spiritual illumination becomes manifest in the world of humanity, when divine instruction and guidance appear, then enlightenment follows, a new spirit is realized within, a new power descends, and a new life is given. It is like the birth from the animal kingdom into the kingdom of man. When man acquires these virtues, the oneness of the world of humanity will be revealed, the banner of international peace will be upraised, equality between all mankind will be realized, and the Orient and Occident will become one. Then will the justice of God become manifest, all humanity will appear as the members of one family, and every member of that family will be consecrated to cooperation and mutual assistance. ('Abdu'l-Bahá, *The Promulgation of Universal Peace,* p. 424.)

Man's evolution is both individual and collective, because of his twofold relationship to himself and to the society in which he lives. Individual evolution starts with the early stages of one's existence. Consciousness too grows with this evolution. (From a letter written on behalf of Shoghi Effendi to an individual believer, dated 14 January 1938, in *Lights of Guidance,* no. 393.)

The long ages of infancy and childhood, through which the human race had to pass, have receded into the background. Humanity is now experiencing the commotions invariably associated with the most turbulent stage of its evolution, the stage of adolescence, when the impetuosity of youth and its vehemence reach their climax, and must gradually be superseded by the calmness, the wisdom, and the maturity that characterize the stage of manhood. Then will the human race reach that stature of ripeness which will enable it to acquire all the powers and capacities upon which its ultimate development must depend. (Shoghi Effendi, *The World Order of Bahá'u'lláh,* p. 201.)

The principle of the Oneness of Mankind, as proclaimed by Bahá'u'lláh, carries with it no more and no less than a solemn assertion that attainment to this final stage in this stupendous evolution is not only necessary but inevitable, that its realization is fast approaching, and that nothing short of a power that is born of God can succeed in establishing it. (Shoghi Effendi, *The World Order of Bahá'u'lláh,* p. 43.)

FORCES EXISTENT IN THE UNIVERSE
Strange and astonishing things exist in the earth but they are hidden from the minds and the understanding of men. These things are capable of changing the whole atmosphere of the earth and their contamination would prove lethal. Great God! We have observed an amazing thing. Lightning or a force similar to it is controlled by an operator and moveth at his command. Immeasurably exalted is the Lord of Power Who hath laid bare that which He purposed through the potency of His weighty and invincible command. (Bahá'u'lláh, *Tablets of Bahá'u'lláh,* p. 69.)

Scientific discoveries have increased material civilization. There is in existence a stupendous force, as yet, happily undiscovered by man. Let us supplicate God, the Beloved, that this force be not discovered by science until spiritual civilization shall dominate the human mind. In the hands of men of lower nature, this power would be able to destroy the whole earth. ('Abdu'l-Bahá, in *Japan Will Turn Ablaze,* p. 51.)

When we observe the phenomena of the universe, we realize that the axis around which life revolves is love, while the axis around which death and destruction revolve is animosity and hatred. Let us view the mineral kingdom. Here we see that if attraction did not exist between the atoms, the composite substance of matter would not be possible. Every existent phenomenon is composed of elements and cellular particles. This is scientifically true and correct. If attraction did not exist between the elements and among the cellular particles, the composition of that phenomenon would never have been possible. ('Abdu'l-Bahá, *The Promulgation of Universal Peace,* p. 374.)

Thus the cohesive and attractive forces in all things lead to the appearance of fruitful results and effects, while estrangement and alienation of things lead to disturbance and annihilation. Through affinity and attraction all living things like plants, animals and men come into existence, while division and discord bring about decomposition and destruction. ('Abdu'l-Bahá, *Selections from the Writings of 'Abdu'l-Bahá,* no. 225.18.)

Love is the cause of God's revelation unto man, the vital bond inherent, in accordance with the divine creation, in the realities of things. . . . Love is the most great law that ruleth this mighty and heavenly cycle, the unique power that bindeth together the divers elements of this material world, the supreme magnetic force that directeth the movements of the spheres in the celestial realms. ('Abdu'l-Bahá, *Selections from the Writings of 'Abdu'l-Bahá,* no. 12.1.)

Similarly in the world of being there exist forces unseen of the eye, such as the force of ether previously mentioned, that cannot be sensed, that cannot be seen. However, from the effects it produceth, that is from its waves and vibrations, light, heat, electricity appear and are made evident. In like manner is the power of growth, of feeling, of understanding, of thought, of memory, of imagination and of discernment; all these inner faculties are unseen of the eye and cannot be sensed, yet all are evident by the effects they produce. ('Abdu'l-Bahá, in *August Forel and the Bahá'í Faith,* p. 19.)

With reference to your question about the "ether," the various definitions of this word as given in the Oxford English Dictionary all refer to a physical reality, for instance, "an element," "a substance," "a medium," all of which imply a physical and objective reality and, as you say, this was the concept posited by nineteenth century scientists to explain the propagation of light waves. It would have been understood in this sense by the audiences whom 'Abdu'l-Bahá was addressing. However, in Chapter XVI of *Some Answered Questions,* 'Abdu'l-Bahá devotes a whole chapter to explaining the difference between things which are "perceptible to the senses" which He calls "objective or sensible," and realities of the "intellect" which have "no outward form and no place," and are "not perceptible to the senses." He gives examples of both "kinds" of "human knowledge." The first kind is obvious and does not need elaboration. To illustrate the second kind the examples He gives are: love, grief, happiness, the power of the intellect, the human spirit and "ethereal matter." (In the original Persian the word "ethereal" is the same as "etheric.") He states clearly that "Even ethereal matter, the forces of which are said in physics to be heat, light, electricity and magnetism, is an intellectual reality, and is not sensible." In other words, the "ether" is a concept arrived at intellectually to explain certain phenomena. In due course, when scientists failed to confirm the physical existence of the "ether" by delicate experiments, they constructed other intellectual concepts to explain the same phenomena. (The Universal House of Justice, *Messages from The Universal House of Justice, 1963–1986,* p. 546.)

Likewise, look into this endless universe: a universal power inevitably existeth, which encompasseth all, directing and regulating all the parts of this infinite creation; and were it not for this Director, this Coordinator, the universe would be flawed and deficient. ('Abdu'l-Bahá, *Selections from the Writings of 'Abdu'l-Bahá,* no. 21.8.)

In like manner consider machinery and workshops and the interaction existing among the various component parts and sections, and how connected they are one with the other. All these relations and interactions, however, are connected with a central power which is their motive force, their pivot and their source. This central power is either the power of steam or the skill of the mastermind.

It hath therefore been made evident and proved that interaction, co-operation and interrelation amongst beings are under the direction and will of a motive Power which is the origin, the motive force and the pivot of all interactions in the universe. ('Abdu'l-Bahá, in *August Forel and the Bahá'í Faith,* p. 23.)

The mind force—whether we call it preexistent or contingent—doth direct and coordinate all the members of the human body, seeing to it that each part or member duly performeth its own special function. If, however, there be some interruption in the power of the mind, all the members will fail to carry out their essential functions, deficiencies will appear in the body and the functioning of its members, and the power will prove ineffective. ('Abdu'l-Bahá, *Selections from the Writings of 'Abdu'l-Bahá,* no. 21.7.)

On the other hand, it is evident and true, though most astounding, that in man there is present this supernatural force or faculty which discovers the realities of things and which possesses the power of idealization or intellection. It is capable of discovering scientific laws. ('Abdu'l-Bahá, *The Promulgation of Universal Peace*, p. 509.)

Consider: according to the law of nature man liveth, moveth and hath his being on earth, yet his soul and mind interfere with the laws thereof, and even as the bird he flieth in the air, saileth speedily upon the seas and as the fish soundeth the deep and discovereth the things therein. Verily this is a grievous defeat inflicted upon the laws of nature.

So is the power of electrical energy: this unruly violent force that cleaveth mountains is yet imprisoned by man within a globe! This is manifestly interfering with the laws of nature. ('Abdu'l-Bahá, in *August Forel and the Bahá'í Faith*, p. 10.)

The greatest power in the realm and range of human existence is spirit—the divine breath which animates and pervades all things. It is manifested throughout creation in different degrees or kingdoms. In the vegetable kingdom it is the augmentative spirit or power of growth, the animus of life and development in plants, trees and organisms of the floral world. In this degree of its manifestation spirit is unconscious of the powers which qualify the kingdom of the animal. The distinctive virtue or plus of the animal is sense perception; it sees, hears, smells, tastes and feels but is incapable, in turn, of conscious ideation or reflection which characterizes and differentiates the human kingdom. ('Abdu'l-Bahá, *The Promulgation of Universal Peace*, pp. 78–79.)

Healing through purely spiritual forces is undoubtedly as inadequate as that which materialist physicians and thinkers vainly seek to obtain by resorting entirely to mechanical devices and methods. The best result can be obtained by combining the two processes: spiritual and physical. (From a letter written on behalf of Shoghi Effendi, dated 12 March 1934, in *The Compilation of Compilations,* vol. I, p. 476.)

The other kind of healing without medicine is through the magnetic force which acts from one body on another and becomes the cause of cure. This force also has only a slight effect. Sometimes one can benefit a sick person by placing one's hand upon his head or upon his heart. Why? Because of the effect of the magnetism, and of the mental impression made upon the sick person, which causes the disease to vanish. But this effect is also very slight and weak. ('Abdu'l-Bahá, *Some Answered Questions,* p. 254.)

Infinity, Space, and Time
The one true God hath everlastingly existed, and will everlastingly continue to exist. His creation, likewise, hath had no beginning, and will have no end. (Bahá'u'lláh, *Gleanings from the Writings of Bahá'u'lláh,* no. 82.10.)

As to thy question concerning the origin of creation. Know assuredly that God's creation hath existed from eternity, and will continue to exist forever. Its beginning hath had no beginning, and its end knoweth no end. (Bahá'u'lláh, *Gleanings from the Writings of Bahá'u'lláh,* no. 82.10.)

O SON OF MAN! Wert thou to speed through the immensity of space and traverse the expanse of heaven, yet thou wouldst find no rest save in submission to Our command and humbleness before Our Face. (Bahá'u'lláh, The Hidden Words, Arabic, no. 40.)

O SON OF MAN! My eternity is My creation, I have created it for thee. Make it the garment of thy temple. My unity is My handiwork; I have wrought it for thee; clothe thyself therewith, that thou mayest be to all eternity the revelation of My everlasting being. (Bahá'u'lláh, The Hidden Words, Arabic, no. 64.)

God is the Ancient, the Almighty; His attributes are infinite. He is God because His light, His sovereignty, is infinite. If He can be limited to human ideas, He is not God. . . . Consider the endless phenomena of His creation. They are infinite; the universe is infinite. Who shall declare its height, its depth and length? It is absolutely infinite. ('Abdu'l-Bahá, *The Promulgation of Universal Peace,* p. 383.)

God is eternal and ancient—not a new God. His sovereignty is of old, not recent—not merely existent these five or six thousand years. This infinite universe is from everlasting. ('Abdu'l-Bahá, *The Promulgation of Universal Peace,* p. 219.)

It is, therefore, evident that inasmuch as the reality of Divinity is without a beginning, creation is also without a beginning. This is as clear as the sun. When we contemplate this vast machinery of omnipresent power, perceive this illimitable space and its innumerable worlds, it will become evident to us that the lifetime of this infinite creation is more than six thousand years; nay, it is very, very ancient. ('Abdu'l-Bahá, *The Promulgation of Universal Peace,* p. 653.)

All divine philosophers and men of wisdom and understanding, when observing these endless beings, have considered that in this great and infinite universe all things end in the mineral kingdom, that the outcome of the mineral kingdom is the vegetable kingdom, the outcome of the vegetable kingdom is the animal kingdom and the outcome of the animal kingdom the world of man. The consummation of this limitless universe with all its grandeur and glory hath been man himself. ('Abdu'l-Bahá, in *August Forel and the Bahá'í Faith,* p. 13.)

Observe that the body of man is confined to a small place; it covers only two spans of earth. But the spirit and mind of man travel to all countries and regions—even through the limitless space of the heavens—surround all that exists, and make discoveries in the exalted spheres and infinite distances. This is because the spirit has no place; it is placeless; and for the spirit the earth and the heaven are as one since it makes discoveries in both. But the body is limited to a place and does not know that which is beyond it. ('Abdu'l-Bahá, *Some Answered Questions,* p. 241.)

For in this universe of God, which appears in the most complete perfection, beauty and grandeur, the luminous stars of the material universe are innumerable! Then we must reflect how limitless and infinite are the spiritual worlds, which are the essential foundation. "Take heed ye who are endued with discernment." ('Abdu'l-Bahá, *Some Answered Questions,* p. 287.)

In the world of God there is no past, no future and no present; all are one. So when Christ said, "In the beginning was the Word"—that means it was, is and shall be; for in the world of God there is no time. Time has sway over creatures but not over God. For example, in the prayer He says, "Hallowed be Thy name"; the meaning is that Thy name was, is and shall be hallowed. Morning, noon and evening are related to this earth, but in the sun there is neither morning, noon nor evening. ('Abdu'l-Bahá, *Some Answered Questions,* p. 156.)

Those who have passed on through death, have a sphere of their own. It is not removed from ours; their work, the work of the Kingdom, is ours; but it is sanctified from what we call "time and place." Time with us is measured by the sun. When there is no more sunrise, and no more sunset, that kind of time does not exist for man. ('Abdu'l-Bahá, *'Abdu'l-Bahá in London,* p. 95.)

You use the expression "till time ends." This is misleading, for there is no end to time. The Guardian suggests that you should either use the term used in the Íqán "till the end that has no end," or express it in such a manner that would give the idea that time has no end. (From a letter written on behalf of Shoghi Effendi, dated 12 November 1933, in *The Unfolding Destiny of the British Bahá'í Community,* p. 432.)

NATURE AND MAN

I am well aware, O my Lord, that I have been so carried away by the clear tokens of Thy loving-kindness, and so completely inebriated with the wine of Thine utterance, that whatever I behold I readily discover that it maketh Thee known unto me, and it remindeth me of Thy signs, and of Thy tokens, and of Thy testimonies. By Thy glory! Every time I lift up mine eyes unto Thy heaven, I call to mind Thy highness and Thy loftiness, and Thine incomparable glory and greatness; and every time I turn my gaze to Thine earth, I am made to recognize the evidences of Thy power and the tokens of Thy bounty. And when I behold the sea, I find that it speaketh to me of Thy majesty, and of the potency of Thy might, and of Thy sovereignty and Thy grandeur. And at whatever time I contemplate the mountains, I am led to discover the ensigns of Thy victory and the standards of Thine omnipotence.

I swear by Thy might, O Thou in Whose grasp are the reins of all mankind, and the destinies of the nations! I am so inflamed by my love for Thee, and so inebriated with the wine of Thy oneness, that I can hear from the whisper of the winds the sound of Thy glorification and praise, and can recognize in the murmur of the waters the voice that proclaimeth Thy virtues and Thine attributes, and can apprehend from the rustling of the leaves the mysteries that have been irrevocably ordained by Thee in Thy realm. (Bahá'u'lláh, *Prayers and Meditations by Bahá'u'lláh,* pp. 271–72.)

Say: Nature in its essence is the embodiment of My Name, the Maker, the Creator. Its manifestations are diversified by varying causes, and in this diversity there are signs for men of discernment. Nature is God's Will and is its expression in and through the contingent world. It is a dispensation of Providence ordained by the Ordainer, the All-Wise. Were anyone to affirm that it is the Will of God as manifested in the world of being, no one should question this assertion. It is endowed with a power whose reality men of learning fail to grasp. Indeed a man of insight can perceive naught therein save the effulgent splendor of Our Name, the Creator. Say: This is an existence which knoweth no decay, and Nature itself is lost in bewilderment before its revelations, its compelling evidences and its effulgent glory which have encompassed the universe. (Bahá'u'lláh, *Tablets of Bahá'u'lláh,* p. 141.)

The phenomenal world is entirely subject to the rule and control of natural law. These myriad suns, satellites and heavenly bodies throughout endless space are all captives of nature. They cannot transgress in a single point or particular the fixed laws which govern the physical universe. The sun in its immensity, the ocean in its vastness are incapable of violating these universal laws. All phenomenal beings—the plants in their kingdom, even the animals with their intelligence—are nature's subjects and captives. All live within the bounds of natural law, and nature is the ruler of all except man. ('Abdu'l-Bahá, *The Promulgation of Universal Peace,* p. 22.)

As to the existence of spirit in the mineral: it is indubitable that minerals are endowed with a spirit and life according to the requirements of that stage. This unknown secret, too, hath become known unto the materialists who now maintain that all beings are endowed with life, even as He saith in the Qur'án, "All things are living."

In the vegetable world, too, there is the power of growth, and that power of growth is the spirit. In the animal world there is the sense of feeling, but in the human world there is an all-embracing power. In all the preceding stages the power of reason is absent, but the soul existeth and revealeth itself. The sense of feeling understandeth not the soul, whereas the reasoning power of the mind proveth the existence thereof.

In like manner the mind proveth the existence of an unseen Reality that embraceth all beings, and that existeth and revealeth itself in all stages, the essence whereof is beyond the grasp of the mind. Thus the mineral world understandeth neither the nature nor the perfections of the vegetable world; the vegetable world understandeth not the nature of the animal world, neither the animal world the nature of the reality of man that discovereth and embraceth all things.

The animal is the captive of nature and cannot transgress the rules and laws thereof. In man, however, there is a discovering power that transcendeth the world of nature and controlleth and interfereth with the laws thereof. For instance, all minerals, plants and animals are captives of nature. The sun itself with all its majesty is so subservient to nature that it hath no will of its own and cannot deviate a hair's-breadth from the laws thereof. In like manner all other beings, whether of the mineral, the vegetable or the animal world, cannot deviate from the laws of nature, nay, all are the slaves thereof. Man, however, though in body the captive of nature is yet free in his mind and soul, and hath the mastery over nature.

Consider: according to the law of nature man liveth, moveth and hath his being on earth, yet his soul and mind interfere with the laws thereof, and even as the bird he flieth in the air, saileth speedily upon the seas and as the fish soundeth the deep and discovereth the things therein. Verily this is a grievous defeat inflicted upon the laws of nature. . . .

In fine, that inner faculty in man, unseen of the eye, wresteth the sword from the hands of nature, and giveth it a grievous blow. All other beings, however great, are bereft of such perfections. Man hath the powers of will and understanding, but nature hath them not. Nature is constrained, man is free. Nature is bereft of understanding, man understandeth. Nature is unaware of past events, but man is aware of them. Nature forecasteth not the future; man by his discerning power seeth that which is to come. Nature hath no consciousness of itself, man knoweth about all things.

Should any one suppose that man is but a part of the world of nature, and he being endowed with these perfections, these being but manifestations of the world of nature, and thus nature is the originator of these perfections and is not deprived therefrom, to him we make reply and say: the part dependeth upon the whole; the part cannot possess perfections whereof the whole is deprived.

By nature is meant those inherent properties and necessary relations derived from the realities of things. And these realities of things, though in the utmost diversity, are yet intimately connected one with the other. For these diverse realities an all-unifying agency is needed that shall link them all one to the other. For instance, the various organs and members, the parts and elements, that constitute the body of man, though at variance, are yet all connected one with the other by that all-unifying agency known as the human soul, that causeth them to function in perfect harmony and with absolute regularity, thus making the continuation of life possible. The human body, however, is utterly unconscious of that all-unifying agency, and yet acteth with regularity and dischargeth its functions according to its will. ('Abdu'l-Bahá, in *August Forel and the Bahá'í Faith,* pp. 9–13.)

When 'Abdu'l-Bahá says man breaks the laws of nature, He means we shape nature to meet our own needs, as no animal does. Animals adapt themselves to better fit in with and benefit from their environment. But men both surmount and change environment. Likewise when He says nature is devoid of memory He means memory as we have it, not the strange memory of inherited habits which animals so strikingly possess. (From a letter written on behalf of Shoghi Effendi, dated 7 June 1946, in *Arohanui: Letters to New Zealand,* p. 85.)

It is evident and manifest that man is capable of breaking nature's laws. How does he accomplish it? Through a spirit with which God has endowed him at creation. This is a proof that the spirit of man differentiates and distinguishes him above all the lower kingdoms. It is this spirit to which the verse in the Old Testament refers when it states, "And God said, Let us make man in our image, after our likeness." The spirit of man alone penetrates the realities of God and partakes of the divine bounties.

This great power must evidently be differentiated from the physical body or temple in which it is manifested. Observe and understand how this human body changes; nevertheless, the spirit of man remains ever in the same condition. . . .

Furthermore, all phenomena are subject to changes from one condition to another, and the revolution caused by this transformation produces a form of nonexistence. For instance, when a man is transformed from the human kingdom to the mineral, we say that he is dead, for he has relinquished the physical form of man and assumed the condition of the mineral substances. This transformation or transmutation is called death. . . .

Again, according to natural philosophy it is an assured fact that single or simple elements are indestructible. As nature is indestructible, every simple element of nature is lasting and permanent. . . .

If an elementary substance is possessed of immortality, how can the human spirit or reality, which is wholly above combination and composition, be destroyed? Nay, rather, that spirit, which is all in all, is a unit and not a compound. Its destruction, therefore, is not possible. The spirit of man transcends the qualities and attributes of any natural element. It is greater in attributes than gold, silver or iron, which are single elements and indestructible. As they are free from destruction and qualified with permanence, how much more so is the human spirit free and immortal. ('Abdu'l-Bahá, *The Promulgation of Universal Peace,* pp. 361–63.)

And just as the composition, the formation, and growth and development of the physical body have come about by degrees, so too must its decomposition and dispersal be gradual. If the disintegration be rapid, this will cause an overlapping and a slackening in the chain of transferences, and this discontinuity will impair the universal relationships within the chain of created things.

For example, this elemental human body hath come forth from the mineral, the vegetable and the animal worlds, and after its death will be entirely changed into microscopic animal organisms; and according to the divine order and the driving forces of nature, these minute creatures will have an effect on the life of the universe, and will pass into other forms.

Now, if you consign this body to the flames, it will pass immediately into the mineral kingdom and will be kept back from its natural journey through the chain of all created things.

The elemental body, following death, and its release from its composite life, will be transformed into separate components and minuscule animals; and even though it will now be deprived of its composite life in human form, still the animal life is in it, and it is not entirely bereft of life. If, however, it be burned, it will turn into ashes and minerals, and once it has become mineral, it must inexorably journey onward to the vegetable kingdom, so that it may rise to the animal world. That is what is described as an overleap.

In short, the composition and decomposition, the gathering and scattering and journeying of all creatures must proceed according to the natural order, divine rule and the most great law of God, so that no marring nor impairment may affect the essential relationships which arise out of the inner realities of created things. This is why, according to the law of God, we are bidden to bury the dead. ('Abdu'l-Bahá, in Marzieh Gail, *Summon Up Remembrance,* pp. 174–76.)

When we consider existence, we see that the mineral, vegetable, animal and human worlds are all in need of an educator.

If the earth is not cultivated, it becomes a jungle where useless weeds grow; but if a cultivator comes and tills the ground, it produces crops which nourish living creatures. It is evident, therefore, that the soil needs the cultivation of the farmer. Consider the trees: if they remain without a cultivator, they will be fruitless, and without fruit they are useless; but if they receive the care of a gardener, these same barren trees become fruitful, and through cultivation, fertilization and engrafting the trees which had bitter fruits yield sweet fruits. These are rational proofs; in this age the peoples of the world need the arguments of reason.

The same is true with respect to animals: notice that when the animal is trained it becomes domestic, and also that man, if he is left without education, becomes bestial, and, moreover, if left under the rule of nature, becomes lower than an animal, whereas if he is educated he becomes an angel. ('Abdu'l-Bahá, *Some Answered Questions,* p. 7.)

A blade of grass severed from the root may live an hour, whereas a human body deprived of its forces may die in one minute. But in the proportion that the human body is weak, the spirit of man is strong. It can control natural phenomena; it is a supernatural power which transcends all contingent beings. It has immortal life, which nothing can destroy or pervert. If all the kingdoms of life arise against the immortal spirit of man and seek its destruction, this immortal spirit, singly and alone, can withstand their attacks in fearless firmness and resolution because it is indestructible and empowered with supreme natural virtues. For this reason we say that the spirit of man can penetrate and discover the realities of all things, can solve the secrets and mysteries of all created objects. While living upon the earth, it discovers the stars and their satellites; it travels underground, finds the metals in their hidden depths and unlocks the secrets of geological ages. It can cross the abysses of interstellar space and discover the motion of inconceivably distant suns. How wonderful it is! ('Abdu'l-Bahá, *The Promulgation of Universal Peace,* p. 368.)

Each kingdom of creation is endowed with its necessary complement of attributes and powers. The mineral possesses inherent virtues of its own kingdom in the scale of existence. The vegetable possesses the qualities of the mineral plus an augmentative virtue, or power of growth. The animal is endowed with the virtues of both the mineral and vegetable plane plus the power of intellect. The human kingdom is replete with the perfections of all the kingdoms below it with the addition of powers peculiar to man alone. Man is, therefore, superior to all the creatures below him, the loftiest and most glorious being of creation. Man is the microcosm; and the infinite universe, the macrocosm. The mysteries of the greater world, or macrocosm, are expressed or revealed in the lesser world, the microcosm. The tree, so to speak, is the greater world, and the seed in its relation to the tree is the lesser world. But the whole of the great tree is potentially latent and hidden in the little seed. When this seed is planted and cultivated, the tree is revealed. Likewise, the greater world, the macrocosm, is latent and miniatured in the lesser world, or microcosm, of man. This constitutes the universality or perfection of virtues potential in mankind. Therefore, it is said that man has been created in the image and likeness of God. ('Abdu'l-Bahá, *The Promulgation of Universal Peace,* p. 95.)

Chapter Six:

Summary

The Lord of all mankind hath fashioned this human realm to be a Garden of Eden, an earthly paradise. If, as it must, it findeth the way to harmony and peace, to love and mutual trust, it will become a true abode of bliss, a place of manifold blessings and unending delights. Therein shall be revealed the excellence of humankind, therein shall the rays of the Sun of Truth shine forth on every hand. ('Abdu'l-Bahá, *Selections from the Writings of 'Abdu'l-Bahá*, no. 220.1.)

Two calls to success and prosperity are being raised from the heights of the happiness of mankind. . . .

The one is the call of civilization, of the progress of the material world. This pertaineth to the world of phenomena, promoteth the principles of material achievement, and is the trainer for the physical accomplishments of mankind. It compriseth the laws, regulations, arts and sciences through which the world of humanity hath developed; laws and regulations which are the outcome of lofty ideals and the result of sound minds, and which have stepped forth into the arena of existence through the efforts of the wise and cultured in past and subsequent ages. The propagator and executive power of this call is just government.

The other is the soul-stirring call of God, Whose spiritual teachings are safeguards of the everlasting glory, the eternal happiness and illumination of the world of humanity, and cause attributes of mercy to be revealed in the human world and the life beyond. . . .

However, until material achievements, physical accomplishments and human virtues are reinforced by spiritual perfections, luminous qualities and characteristics of mercy, no fruit or result shall issue therefrom, nor will the happiness of the world of humanity, which is the ultimate aim, be attained. For although, on the one hand, material achievements and the development of the physical world produce prosperity, which exquisitely manifests its intended aims, on the other hand dangers, severe calamities and violent afflictions are imminent. . . .

Praise be to God, throughout succeeding centuries and ages the call of civilization hath been raised, the world of humanity hath been advancing and progressing day by day, various countries have been developing by leaps and bounds, and material improvements have increased, until the world of existence obtained universal capacity to receive the spiritual teachings and to hearken to the Divine Call. The suckling babe passeth through various physical stages, growing and developing at every stage, until its body reacheth the age of maturity. Having arrived at this stage it acquireth the capacity to manifest spiritual and intellectual perfections. The lights of comprehension, intelligence and knowledge become perceptible in it and the powers of its soul unfold. Similarly, in the contingent world, the human species hath undergone progressive physical changes and, by a slow process, hath scaled the ladder of civilization, realizing in itself the wonders, excellencies and gifts of humanity in their most glorious form, until it gained the capacity to express the splendors of spiritual perfections and divine ideals and became capable of hearkening to the call of God. Then at last the call of the Kingdom was raised, the spiritual virtues and perfections were revealed, the Sun of Reality dawned, and the teachings of the Most Great Peace, of the oneness of the world of humanity and of the universality of men, were promoted. We hope that the effulgence of these rays shall become more and more intense, and the ideal virtues more resplendent, so that the goal of this universal human process will be attained and the love of God will appear in the utmost grace and beauty and bedazzle all hearts.

O ye beloved of God! Know ye, verily, that the happiness of mankind lieth in the unity and the harmony of the human race, and that spiritual and material developments are conditioned upon love and amity among all men. ('Abdu'l-Bahá, *Selections from the Writings of 'Abdu'l-Bahá*, no. 225.1–10.)

In the estimation of historians this radiant century is equivalent to one hundred centuries of the past. If comparison be made with the sum total of all former human achievements, it will be found that the discoveries, scientific advancement and material civilization of this present century have equaled, yea far exceeded the progress and outcome of one hundred former centuries. The production of books and compilations of literature alone bears witness that the output of the human mind in this century has been greater and more enlightening than all the past centuries together. It is evident, therefore, that this century is of paramount importance. Reflect upon the miracles of accomplishment which have already characterized it: the discoveries in every realm of human research. Inventions, scientific knowledge, ethical reforms and regulations established for the welfare of humanity, mysteries of nature explored, invisible forces brought into visibility and subjection—a veritable wonder-world of new phenomena and conditions heretofore unknown to man now open to his uses and further investigation. . . . What a wonderful century this is! It is an age of universal reformation. Laws and statutes of civil and federal governments are in process of change and transformation. Sciences and arts are being molded anew. Thoughts are metamorphosed. The foundations of human society are changing and strengthening. Today sciences of the past are useless. The Ptolemaic system of astronomy and numberless other systems and theories of scientific and philosophical explanation are discarded, known to be false and worthless. Ethical precedents and principles cannot be applied to the needs of the modern world. Thoughts and theories of past ages are fruitless now. Thrones and governments are crumbling and falling. All conditions and requisites of the past unfitted and inadequate for the present time are undergoing radical reform. It is evident, therefore, that counterfeit and spurious religious teaching, antiquated forms of belief and ancestral imitations which are at variance with the foundations of divine reality must also pass away and be reformed. They must be abandoned and new conditions be recognized. The morals of humanity must undergo change. New remedies and solutions for human problems must be adopted. Human intellects themselves must change and be subject to the universal reformation. Just as the thoughts and hypotheses of past ages are fruitless today, likewise dogmas and codes of human invention are obsolete and barren of product in religion. Nay, it is true that they are the cause of enmity and conducive to strife in the world of humanity; war and bloodshed proceed from them, and the oneness of mankind finds no recognition in their observance. Therefore, it is our duty in this radiant century to investigate the essentials of divine religion, seek the realities underlying the oneness of the world of humanity and discover the source of fellowship and agreement which will unite mankind in the heavenly bond of love. . . . For if we remain fettered and restricted by human inventions and dogmas, day by day the world of mankind will be degraded, day by day warfare and strife will increase and satanic forces converge toward the destruction of the human race. ('Abdu'l-Bahá, *The Promulgation of Universal Peace,* pp. 198–200.)

The unity of the human race, as envisaged by Bahá'-
u'lláh, implies the establishment of a world commonwealth in which all nations, races, creeds and classes
are closely and permanently united, and in which
the autonomy of its state members and the personal
freedom and initiative of the individuals that compose them are definitely and completely safeguarded.
This commonwealth must, as far as we can visualize
it, consist of a world legislature, whose members will,
as the trustees of the whole of mankind, ultimately
control the entire resources of all the component nations, and will enact such laws as shall be required to
regulate the life, satisfy the needs and adjust the relationships of all races and peoples. A world executive,
backed by an international Force, will carry out the
decisions arrived at, and apply the laws enacted by,
this world legislature, and will safeguard the organic
unity of the whole commonwealth. A world tribunal
will adjudicate and deliver its compulsory and final
verdict in all and any disputes that may arise between
the various elements constituting this universal system. A mechanism of world inter-communication will
be devised, embracing the whole planet, freed from
national hindrances and restrictions, and functioning with marvellous swiftness and perfect regularity.
A world metropolis will act as the nerve center of a
world civilization, the focus towards which the unifying forces of life will converge and from which its
energizing influences will radiate. A world language
will either be invented or chosen from among the ex-

isting languages and will be taught in the schools of all the federated nations as an auxiliary to their mother tongue. A world script, a world literature, a uniform and universal system of currency, of weights and measures, will simplify and facilitate intercourse and understanding among the nations and races of mankind. In such a world society, science and religion, the two most potent forces in human life, will be reconciled, will cooperate, and will harmoniously develop. The press will, under such a system, while giving full scope to the expression of the diversified views and convictions of mankind, cease to be mischievously manipulated by vested interests, whether private or public, and will be liberated from the influence of contending governments and peoples. The economic resources of the world will be organized, its sources of raw materials will be tapped and fully utilized, its markets will be coordinated and developed, and the distribution of its products will be equitably regulated.

National rivalries, hatreds, and intrigues will cease, and racial animosity and prejudice will be replaced by racial amity, understanding and cooperation. The causes of religious strife will be permanently removed, economic barriers and restrictions will be completely abolished, and the inordinate distinction between classes will be obliterated. Destitution on the one hand, and gross accumulation of ownership on the other, will disappear. The enormous energy dissipated and wasted on war, whether economic or political, will be consecrated to such ends as will extend the range of human inventions and technical development, to the increase of the productivity of mankind, to the extermination of disease, to the extension of scientific research, to the raising of the standard of physical health, to the sharpening and refinement of the human brain, to the exploitation of the unused and unsuspected resources of the planet, to the prolongation of human life, and to the furtherance of any other agency that can stimulate the intellectual, the moral, and spiritual life of the entire human race.

A world federal system, ruling the whole earth and exercising unchallengeable authority over its unimaginably vast resources, blending and embodying the ideals of both the East and the West, liberated from the curse of war and its miseries, and bent on the exploitation of all the available sources of energy on the surface of the planet, a system in which Force is made the servant of Justice, whose life is sustained by its universal recognition of one God and by its allegiance to one common Revelation—such is the goal towards which humanity, impelled by the unifying forces of life, is moving. (Shoghi Effendi, *The World Order of Bahá'u'lláh,* p. 203.)

Bahá'u'lláh found the world in a "strange sleep." But what a disturbance His coming has unloosed! The peoples of the earth had been separated, many parts of the human race socially and spiritually isolated. But the world of humanity today bears little resemblance to that which Bahá'u'lláh left a century ago.

Unbeknownst to the great majority, His influence permeates all living beings. Indeed, no domain of life remains unaffected. In the burgeoning energy, the magnified perspectives, the heightened global consciousness; in the social and political turbulence, the fall of kingdoms, the emancipation of nations, the intermixture of cultures, the clamour for development; in the agitation over the extremes of wealth and poverty, the acute concern over the abuse of the environment, the leap of consciousness regarding the rights of women; in the growing tendency towards ecumenism, the increasing call for a new world order; in the astounding advances in the realms of science, technology, literature and the arts—in all this tumult, with its paradoxical manifestations of chaos and order, integration and disintegration, are the signs of His power as World Reformer, the proof of His claim as Divine Physician, the truth of His Word as the All-Knowing Counsellor.

Bahá'u'lláh wrote voluminously about the purpose of this mysterious force and its transformative effects, but the essence can be drawn from these few perspicuous words: "Through the movement of Our Pen of Glory We have, at the bidding of the Omnipotent Ordainer, breathed a new life into every human frame, and instilled into every word a fresh potency. All created things proclaim the evidences of this worldwide regeneration." And again: "A new life is, in this age, stirring within all the peoples of the earth; and yet none hath discovered its cause or perceived its motive." And yet again: "He Who is the Unconditioned is come, in the clouds of light, that He may quicken all created things with the breezes of His Name, the Most Merciful, and unify the world, and gather all men around this Table which hath been sent down from heaven." (The Universal House of Justice, May 1992, tribute to Bahá'u'lláh on the occasion of the Centenary Commemoration at Bahji of the Ascension of Bahá'u'lláh, in *Science and Religion,* pp. 5–6.)

BIBLIOGRAPHY

WORKS OF BAHÁ'U'LLÁH

Epistle to the Son of the Wolf. 1st pocket-size ed. Translated
by Shoghi Effendi. Wilmette, IL: Bahá'í Publishing
Trust, 1988.

Gleanings from the Writings of Bahá'u'lláh. Translated by
Shoghi Effendi. Wilmette, IL: Bahá'í Publishing, 2005.

The Hidden Words. Translated by Shoghi Effendi. Wilmette, IL: Bahá'í Publishing, 2002.

The Kitáb-i-Aqdas: The Most Holy Book. 1st pocket-size ed.
Wilmette, IL: Bahá'í Publishing Trust, 1993.

The Kitáb-i-Íqán: The Book of Certitude. Translated by
Shoghi Effendi. Wilmette, IL: Bahá'í Publishing, 2003.

Prayers and Meditations. Translated by Shoghi Effendi. 1st
pocket-size ed. Wilmette, IL: Bahá'í Publishing Trust,
1987.

Tablets of Bahá'u'lláh revealed after the Kitáb-i-Aqdas. Compiled by the Research Department of the Universal
House of Justice. Translated by Habib Taherzadeh et
al. Wilmette, IL: 1988.

WORKS OF 'ABDU'L-BAHÁ

*'Abdu'l-Bahá in London: Addresses and Notes of Conversa-
tions.* London: Bahá'í Publishing Trust, 1982.

Paris Talks: Addresses Given By 'Abdu'l-Bahá in Paris in 1911.
Wilmette, IL: Bahá'í Publishing, 2011.

The Promulgation of Universal Peace: Talks Delivered by 'Abdu'l-Bahá during His Visit to the United States and Canada in 1912. Compiled by Howard MacNutt. Wilmette, IL: Bahá'í Publishing, 2012.

Selections from the Writings of 'Abdu'l-Bahá. Compiled by the Research Department of the Universal House of Justice. Translated by a Committee at the Bahá'í World Center and Marzieh Gail. Wilmette, IL: Bahá'í Publishing, 2010.

Some Answered Questions. Compiled and translated by Laura Clifford Barney. 1st pocket-size ed. Wilmette, IL: Bahá'í Publishing Trust, 1984.

WORKS OF SHOGHI EFFENDI

Arohanui: Letters from Shoghi Effendi to New Zealand. Suva, Fiji: Bahá'í Publishing Trust, 1982.

God Passes By. New ed. Wilmette, IL: Bahá'í Publishing Trust, 1974.

High Endeavours: Messages to Alaska. [n.p.]: Bahá'í Publishing Trust, 1976.

The Light of Divine Guidance: The Messages from the Guardian of the Bahá'í Faith to the Bahá'ís of Germany and Austria. Hofheim-Langenhain, Germany: Bahá'í-Verlag, 1982.

Messages to the Antipodes: Communications from Shoghi Effendi to the Bahá'í Communities of Australasia. Mona Vale, Australia: Bahá'í Publications Australia, 1987.

The Unfolding Destiny of the British Bahá'í Community: The Messages from the Guardian of the Bahá'í Faith to the Bahá'ís of the British Isles. London: Bahá'í Publishing Trust, 1981.

The World Order of Bahá'u'lláh: Selected Letters. 1st pocket-size ed. Wilmette, IL: Bahá'í Publishing Trust, 1991.

WORKS OF THE
UNIVERSAL HOUSE OF JUSTICE

Messages from the Universal House of Justice, 1963–1986: The Third Epoch of the Formative Age. Compiled by Geoffry Marks. Wilmette, IL: Bahá'í Publishing Trust, 1996.

Messages from the Universal House of Justice, 1968–1973. Haifa: Bahá'í World Center, 1973.

The Promise of World Peace: To the Peoples of the World. Wilmette, IL: Bahá'í Publishing Trust, 1985.

To the World's Religious Leaders: A Message from the Universal House of Justice. Wilmette, IL: Bahá'í Publishing Trust, 2002.

COMPILATIONS OF BAHÁ'Í WRITINGS

The Compilation of Compilations: Prepared by the Universal House of Justice, 1963–1990. 2 vols. Australia: Bahá'í Publications Australia, 1991.

Extracts from the Writings of Bahá'u'lláh and 'Abdu'l-Bahá and from the Letters of Shoghi Effendi and the Universal House of Justice on Scholarship. Prepared by the Research Department of the Universal House of Justice. Haifa: Bahá'í World Center, 1995.

Issues Related to the Study of the Bahá'í Faith: Extracts from Letters Written on Behalf of the Universal House of Justice. Haifa: Bahá'í World Center, 1992.

Lights of Guidance: A Bahá'í Reference File. Compiled by Helen Hornby. New ed. New Dehli, India: Bahá'í Publishing Trust, 1994.

The Pupil of the Eye: African Americans in World Order of Bahá'u' lláh: Selections from the Writings of Bahá'u'lláh, the Bab, 'Abdu'l-Bahá, Shoghi Effendi, and the Universal House of Justice. Compiled by Bonnie J. Taylor. 2nd ed. Rivera Beach, Florida: Palabra Publication, 1998.

Quotations on Science and Religion. Prepared by the Research Department of the Universal House of Justice. Haifa: Bahá'í World Center, 1997.

OTHER WORKS

Gail, Marzieh. *Summon Up Remembrance.* Oxford: George Ronald, 1987.

Bahá'í
PUBLISHING

Bahá'í Publishing and the Bahá'í Faith

Bahá'í Publishing produces books based on the teachings of the Bahá'í Faith. Founded over 160 years ago, the Bahá'í Faith has spread to some 235 nations and territories and is now accepted by more than five million people. The word "Bahá'í" means "follower of Bahá'u'lláh." Bahá'u'lláh, the founder of the Bahá'í Faith, asserted that He is the Messenger of God for all of humanity in this day. The cornerstone of His teachings is the establishment of the spiritual unity of humankind, which will be achieved by personal transformation and the application of clearly identified spiritual principles. Bahá'ís also believe that there is but one religion and that all the Messengers of God—among them Abraham, Zoroaster, Moses, Krishna, Buddha, Jesus, and Muḥammad—have progressively revealed its nature. Together, the world's great religions are expressions of a single, unfolding divine plan. Human beings, not God's Messengers, are the source of religious divisions, prejudices, and hatreds.

The Bahá'í Faith is not a sect or denomination of another religion, nor is it a cult or a social movement. Rather, it is a globally recognized independent world religion founded on new books of scripture revealed by Bahá'u'lláh.

Bahá'í Publishing is an imprint of the National Spiritual Assembly of the Bahá'ís of the United States.

For more information about the Bahá'í Faith,
or to contact Bahá'ís near you,
visit http://www.bahai.us/
or call
1-800-22-UNITE

Other Books Available from Bahá'í Publishing

BLESSED IS THE SPOT
Bahá'u'lláh
Illustrated by Constance von Kitzing
$12.00 US / $14.00 CAN
Paper Over Board
ISBN 978-1-61851-048-8

A beautifully illustrated prayer book for children; a perfect book for the whole family to treasure.

Blessed is the Spot is a simple and beautiful prayer book for children. Illustrated with warm and inviting imagery by Constanze von Kitzing, whose work strikes the perfect balance between playful and reverent, the book contains a single prayer from the writings of the Bahá'í Faith. The prayer has long been loved and cherished by the Bahá'í community for its exquisite yet accessible words, and it is hoped that many new readers, both children and parents alike, will fall in love with it and find inspiration in its uplifting words.

DREAMS OF DESTINY IN THE BÁBÍ AND BAHÁ'Í FAITHS

Amir Badiei

$17.00 US / $19.00 CAN

Trade Paper

ISBN 978-1-61851-045-7

A new exploration of the significance of the role of dreams in almost all the religions and cultures of the world, with a focus on the history of the Bahá'í Faith.

The history of the Bahá'í Faith is full of fascinating stories related to the influence of dreams. Many people who associated with the Báb, the Herald of the Faith; Bahá'u'lláh, the Prophet-Founder; 'Abdu'l-Bahá, the Center of His Covenant; and Shoghi Effendi, the Guardian of the Faith had dreams that compelled them to investigate the Bahá'í teachings and seek out religious truth for themselves. Some ended up traveling long distances, enduring formidable hardships, and undergoing severe tests to find the answers to their questions. In *Dreams of Destiny in the Bábí and Bahá'í Faiths,* Dr. Amir Badiei has compiled the accounts of dreams from Bahá'í history and how they impacted the people who experienced them. All of the dreamers were changed by their experiences, and all discovered more about themselves through the process of investigating their dreams. It is hoped that this compilation will inspire others who have had similar dreams to start their own journey toward self-discovery.

WAVE WATCHER
Craig Alan Johnson
$14.00 US / $16.00 CAN
Trade Paper
ISBN 978-1-61851-046-4

A thoughtful and beautifully written young-adult novel about a young boy growing up and dealing with a tragic event that shapes his life and understanding of the world.

Twelve-year-old Ray can't sleep. Everyone thinks it's because of bad dreams, but it's not. His thoughts keep him awake—especially tonight, exactly one year after the devastating event that changed his life forever. The gifted young writer's pen has been silent since then, stilled by the shock. Tonight Ray will break the silence. He will begin to write again. Looking back on his short life, he will tell the story of who he is and try to make sense of the patterns that once seemed so sure. In the process he will come to see how a broken-down house, a brother with only one lung, the Mozart his mother plays on the piano, his father's novel, a whisper in a cave, a grandmother who prays at midnight, and a man-eating Chihuahua have helped him make sense of the patterns in his life. *Wave Watcher* is a story about what it means to be an everyday hero, and what it means to be human. Author Craig Johnson's novel, written for a young adult audience, will make us laugh, cry, hope, and strive to live as fully as possible.

SPIRIT OF FAITH
LIFE AFTER DEATH
Bahá'í Publishing
$12.00 US / $14.00 CAN
Hardcover
ISBN 978-1-61851-047-1

The seventh book in the Spirit of Faith series focuses on the subject of life after death and the immortality of the human soul.

Spirit of Faith: Life After Death is a compilation of writings and prayers that explore the topic of death and the transition from this life to the worlds beyond our world. Many of the writings of the Bahá'í Faith emphasize our limited time on this planet and the importance of our conduct while here. The passages compiled here touch on the immortality of the human soul, the importance of detachment from earthly desires, and the continuation of life in the spiritual worlds of God. Similar to previous titles in this series, this collection of sacred scripture can help define our place within a single, unfolding, divine creation. The *Spirit of Faith* series continues to explore spiritual topics—such as the unity of humanity, the eternal covenant of God, the promise of world peace, and more—by presenting what the central figures of the Bahá'í Faith have written regarding these important topics.